The Richard and
Judy Story

The Richard and Judy Story

Carole Malone

First published in Great Britain in 1996 by
Virgin Books
an imprint of Virgin Publishing Ltd
332 Ladbroke Grove
London W10 5AH

A catalogue record for this book is available from the British Library.

ISBN 1 85227 626 6

Typeset by TW Typesetting, Plymouth, Devon

Printed and bound by
Mackays of Chatham, Lordswood, Chatham, Kent

For Mum, Dad and Nino –
to whom I owe so much more
than a book.

Contents

Illustrations

Acknowledgements

I'd like to thank all those people who took the time and trouble – not to mention a risk – to talk to me. They know who they are. Thanks!

Prologue

Prologue: 1 December 1995

IT WAS FRIDAY MORNING and the last *This Morning* of the week was just 40 minutes away from going on air. Everyone racing round the Albert Dock studio on that bitterly cold morning should have been gearing up for the weekend ahead. Christmas was just three weeks away and evidence of it was already queueing up outside the studio's vast window, as a line of excited children giggled and fidgeted, waiting for Santa's grotto to open next door.

By contrast, the atmosphere inside the studio was fraught with tension. But this was much more than the usual countdown jitters, the edginess that always precedes a live television show. This was a different kind of excitement altogether – the kind that smells of fear. Something big was about to go down at the Dock that morning and it was nothing to do with Santa Claus. You could feel it in the air, which had become thick with expectancy. One or two members of the crew were wandering round whispering. Others stood huddled in corners, worry etched into their faces.

On the surface everything looked normal – dazzling even. The hot studio lights blazed down on the vibrant green, orange and yellow backdrops of the Mediterranean-style set, radiating instant warmth as if to counteract the cold dank day beyond the towering glass walls of the studio. A few people shivered as they looked out on to the murky water of the Dock.

Outside, people walked briskly by the bustling studio, huddled against the cold of the sharp December day. A few momentarily slackened their pace, ignoring the studio guard whose job it was to move on the gawpers. Noses pressed up against the sweeping windows, using frozen hands to shield their eyes against the blinding glare of the studio lights, they peered through the brightness hoping the king and queen of daytime might magically step out of it.

But they didn't. Not that morning.

The rest of the shoppers hurried by determinedly, desperate to make inroads on their Christmas lists. There were, after all, only 24 shopping days left.

Inside the cosy studio, the *This Morning* kitchen was, as usual, alive with frenetic activity. People in colourful aprons were rushing round clutching dishes of meat and fresh vegetables which would soon be transformed into Susan Brookes's dish of the day. The clatter of plates clashed with muffled voices in the cramped kitchen near the studio entrance and soon the smell of some half-cooked Eastern dish wafted in delicious spicy waves through the building and out of it as people opened and closed the doors.

Fred the weatherman, wearing one of his specially hand-knitted jumpers, was steeling himself to go outside and brave the chilly day. It didn't matter how cold it got, Fred still had to jump aboard his floating weather map and perform his daredevil leaps for the cheering crowds who waited every day to see him. Like everyone else, today he looked anxious.

Lee Din, Judy's personal hair and make-up artist, was standing on the edge of the studio floor. Armed with powder and puff, he was waiting for the star to emerge from her dressing room so that he could do some final 'touching up' before she stepped in front of the cameras. Beside him, talking quietly, stood *This Morning*'s elegant programme manager, Geraldine Woods. As always she looked immaculate in one of her exquisitely cut suits. But today she and Lee seemed anxious. All round, production staff, researchers and cameramen were going through the script, working out moves and camera angles.

I had flown up from London that damp Friday morning to do a phone-in about sex and teenage magazines. Earlier in the week, *TV Hits* had run a letter from a sixteen-year-old girl who had said she wanted to know how to perform oral sex on her boyfriend. The magazine's graphic reply had caused a storm in the media. As an old friend of the programme, I had been invited up to Liverpool to speak out against the magazine's liberal stance. Charlotte Owen, the agony aunt from *19*, was to be my opposite number and speak in favour of it. We were both tired, having been up since 6am to make the 7.45 plane from London's Heathrow to Manchester. But there was something about that warm, welcoming studio in the heart of Liverpool's dockland that always made it a pleasure to be there.

From the minute you walked up the cobbled path and in through the heavy blackened doors that led to the studio floor, you immediately felt cheered. The girls who met you from the taxi greeted you like an old friend. The make-up artists were always bright and funny, and had the knack of making even those of us who'd been out on the town the night before, and had bags under our eyes the size of coal sacks, look like we'd just stepped out of a magazine ad.

Down the road in the green room, adjacent to the *This Morning* studio, generous portions of scouse humour were regularly served up with the tea and sandwiches. The show's taxi drivers, Neil, Keith and Peter, whose job it was to ferry guests from Manchester Airport to the studio, were always on hand with a laugh and a bit of Liverpudlian cheek to steady guests who might be suffering from a dose of pre-show jitters.

The people who worked for *This Morning* were usually great fun – but not this particular Friday.

Some of them must have had a premonition of what was about to happen. There'd been talk for months. Rumours about the show moving from Liverpool had started six months before and had now reached fever pitch. There had been talk of *This Morning* moving to Salford Quays, the multi-million pound dock complex just outside Manchester. There were also rumours that it might be going to London. The problem for the staff of *This Morning*, many of whom had worked there since day one of transmission, was the uncertainty.

Because, in their hearts, everyone knew that at some stage the show was going to have to be uprooted from this dockside studio, where it had grown from nothing to the jewel in the crown of daytime TV.

In the eight years *This Morning* had been on air it had gone from strength to strength, in that tiny studio, with barely room to house the essential equipment, let alone the dozens of people who passed through it, day after frantic day. The contribution of Richard and Judy, the two star presenters, was immeasurable, but there was another, less widely appreciated reason for the show's success.

When *This Morning* first went on air on 3 October 1988, a very special spirit manifested itself on that cramped studio floor. It was as if some glorious genie of good will had risen out of the blood, sweat, tears and love of the team who had put it all together, and this blessing had sustained the show ever since. The hard-working and talented production team had forged itself into a tight-knit community of people, and it was that community, together with Richard and Judy, which had taken the show from strength to dazzling strength. On that cheerless December morning, was it to be torn apart for ever?

When Max Gressor, Granada's director of productions, arrived grim-faced on the studio floor at 10am sharp that morning, everyone knew an announcement was imminent. Suddenly the tension that had been hanging in the air like smoke broke into panic.

I was standing on the edge of the floor when Richard Madeley, looking immaculate in a well-cut navy Italian suit and an ice-white shirt worn with a red silk tie, stopped to say 'Hi' as he rushed past. As he bent to plant a welcoming kiss on my cheek, he whispered, 'Hang about, Carole. You're about to hear something that might interest you.'

Seconds later Judy emerged from her dressing room. She looked smart, sharper than usual, in an elegant black designer suit with a swathe of jet satin that had been cut across the front to resemble a waistcoat. She had on the customary stilettos that Richard likes her to wear, sheer black tights and a white satin camisole. She looked different, classier somehow. Was this a portent, a sign of things to come? Judy, whose refreshing lack of vanity had always set her apart from other TV presenters, had finally been persuaded, after months of gentle coaxing from Lee Din, to get rid of her old-fashioned bob in favour of a more layered nineties look. Today she was sporting the glamorous rough-cut style which made her look trendier, more fashionable, younger.

But on this particular morning no one was looking at Judy, now discreetly taking her place by Richard's side. Instead everyone was looking at Max Gressor, standing in the middle of the studio floor ready to address the staff with a carefully prepared statement that would forever change the lives of those listening.

It took less than five minutes for the director of productions to tell the staff – whose loyalty and dedication had catapulted the show to the top of the daytime ratings schedule – that *This Morning* was moving, lock, stock and barrel, to the capital. He thanked them for all their hard work and told them they would be seen individually about their future prospects at a later date.

As shock registered on the faces around him, Gressor's slow, steady voice cut through the silence like a knife. The announcement was delivered unemotionally. He said that from September 1996 the show would be broadcast from a brand-new studio on the banks of the Thames. He tried to reassure the troubled staff that the move didn't necessarily mean job losses but it was clear they didn't believe him. The old hands, some of them union men who had been a powerful force in television until Maggie Thatcher intervened, had heard it all before. They shook their heads in silent disbelief. Until a few years ago they might have been able to stop a move such as this. In Tory Britain 1995 they were powerless against a TV monolith whose prime motivation was money.

Despite his apparent lack of emotion, it must have been a difficult speech for Max Gressor. Eight years before he had been the producer on the first-ever pilot of *This Morning*. He was there right at the beginning in Liverpool, and here he was again, presiding over the end. He tried to reassure the sea of worried faces staring back at him that their jobs were safe. But he knew that, even after years of management training for situations like this, he had not convinced them.

As Max continued his speech, Richard and Judy stood impassively behind him. Silently they listened as details of the plan were relayed to the staff. They'd known about Granada's decision to move the show for months now. It had first been mooted at the Edinburgh Film Festival that summer when their agent, Annie Sweetbaum, had been approached by Granada chiefs who'd asked how the couple would feel if the whole show was moved. The suggestion could not have been entirely unexpected by the two stars, who had made it known that when their present two-year contract came to an end, it could be their last. They'd agreed to the move almost immediately.

Gressor finished his speech and then it was back to work. Having just been told that their lives were about to be turned upside down, the team, in true showbiz tradition, had to go on with the show that people all over Britain were waiting to watch.

For Richard and Judy it was not such a shock. They'd had months to get used to the idea of moving to London. It was a move they'd both sought, each for their own different reasons, though both wanted a change of scene and new challenges. 'We'd have lost them if we hadn't given them London,' one of Granada's top executives said to me that morning. 'We had to do it.'

Rightly or wrongly, Richard and Judy had decided long before that day that London was the natural progression, not just for the show but for their personal careers as well. They both understood that being on the show as a married couple was not a situation that could continue indefinitely. Judy was 48 and perhaps growing a little tired. Richard was 40, full of life and desperate to free himself from the constraints that were keeping him from the one big television mountain he had yet to climb: prime time. Richard wanted big-time, big-money television, and his wife loved and supported him in his ambition. Newspapers, desperate for details of why daytime's top-rated show was moving to the capital, were told that the show's bosses, as well as its two stars, felt that by staying in the north they were missing out on the big-name celebrity guests. Judy had reportedly been furious when heart-throb Tom Cruise had refused to fly to Liverpool because it was too far to travel. Elton John and Mel Gibson were also rumoured to have said no because of the distance involved. Richard himself fuelled the fire when he said the day the move was announced: 'If we want to stay on top, we have to make sure we go where the stars are.'

And that was partly true. When the hottest Hollywood stars hit Britain they rarely set foot outside the capital, with its endless chat shows and star-studded premières. And, if they do make forays into other parts of Britain, it isn't to economically depressed cities like Liverpool – whose only attraction for Americans is the fact that the Beatles were born there – it is to cities like Edinburgh, which not only has 'history' but artistic street cred as well. Because celebrities are tied to tight schedules, timed down to the last minute, few are prepared to spend six hours out of a day travelling to and from Liverpool for the privilege of ten minutes on the coffee slot with Richard and Judy.

But this wasn't a new situation. And, more importantly, it wasn't a situation that had ever affected the ratings. Quite the reverse. Because, apart from a few hairy months during the first year of the BBC's rival programme *Good Morning*, when the ratings were often neck and neck, *This Morning* had consistently gone from strength to strength. Moreover, it was only a few weeks after Granada announced their decision to move the show to London that the BBC threw in the towel and conceded defeat against their ITV rivals. There was no longer any threat from the other side. No need to lure guests with private helicopters and high-class limousines. They had the floor to themselves.

Which is why those closest to Richard and Judy believed that relocation to London was seen primarily as a career move for them. They had talked about leaving *This Morning* 'on a high' in 1996, before moving south to pursue other options. Whether their talk of leaving the show was in the knowledge that Granada would capitulate and do whatever it took to make them stay we will never know, but if it was a gamble it paid off. Between them, the couple held a winning hand. If Granada didn't want to offer them exciting new opportunities in London, there were plenty of TV companies who did.

Richard and Judy were seen to have won the daytime war for Granada in the teeth of strong opposition from the BBC. Their reward was the ability to write their own cheque.

Over the years there had been subtle approaches from other TV companies. The couple knew their worth. But they felt comfortable with Granada; they'd been together a long time. And if Richard and Judy knew their worth, so did the Granada executives. Save for a few odd occasions, the ratings plummeted when Richard and Judy weren't presenting *This Morning*. And ratings meant money. No one was prepared to gamble the millions of pounds that *This Morning* generated in advertising revenue by letting the two people believed to be the reason for it slip through their fingers.

It also made professional and economic sense for Granada to take Richard and Judy to London. They were paying the two stars a lot of money to present what was still just a daytime programme, pulling in a maximum of between 1.5 and 2 million viewers. In London they could work them harder, and get more out of them for their £1.5 million contract. Richard and Judy could be asked to do more programmes, different shows. They could be seen out and about on the celebrity circuit, which would in turn generate positive publicity for Granada but which was impossible while the two of them were working in Liverpool and having to be in the studio by 9am every day.

So it was decided that the show and the two star presenters would move to a brand-new Thameside studio where, on a good day, you can see the dome of St Paul's Cathedral to the right and the Houses of Parliament to the left. No expense was to be spared in the relocation because, in their own sphere, Richard and Judy are the undisputed king and queen. Not only in ratings terms, but salary too. Their contract for £1.5 million makes them two of the most highly paid presenters in British TV. Their superbracket salary puts them on a par with stars like Cilla Black, Michael Barrymore and Anthea Turner.

But Richard and Judy wanted more than money. They craved a foothold in prime time television, a place in TV history among Britain's brightest and glitziest stars.

* * *

At least, that's what Richard craved. For years TV's Mr Smoothie, the man who can talk just as knowledgeably about women's gynaecological problems (especially his wife's) as he can about the intricacies of Norwegian cross stitch, Richard sees himself in a more serious role.

Those who know him say Richard thinks he could be better than many of the present broadcasting heavyweights. It's something he's believed since his days as a rookie reporter at BBC Radio Cumbria.

One colleague who worked with him there, Tony Baker, recalls: 'He'd come into the office some mornings and say, "Did anyone see *Panorama* last night?" None of us had, of course, because we were all young lads and had all been down the pub. But not Richard. He would stay at home studying these guys – their style, their speech, their delivery – and then the next morning he'd say, "What did you think of the way such and such a presenter asked that question?" We'd all shrug our shoulders because it hadn't occurred to any of us to watch how anyone asked a question.

'Richard was alarmingly confident and always maintained he could do it better. And the funny thing was, we all believed him. Even though he was just nineteen, precocious and criticising blokes who'd been presenting for longer than he'd been alive, we still thought he probably *could* be better than most of them.'

Richard Madeley had always been driven by ambition, but his wife is different. Judy Finnigan is commonly believed to be her husband's intellectual superior. Her mind is sharper, more incisive than Richard's, yet everything in Judy's career has 'just happened'. She has never sought stardom or celebrity in the way that her husband has, yet she has continually been cast in the role of reluctant star.

There were those in the newsroom of *Granada Reports* in Manchester, where the couple first met, who were jealous of the pretty blonde with the piercing blue eyes who always seemed to be in the right place at the right time; the girl who came back to work after taking three years out to spend time with her twin boys and, just a few weeks after her return, landed the prize job of presenting a nightly magazine programme.

For most women, taking three years out in the fast-moving world of television would almost certainly have spelt death in career terms. But not for Judy. Much to some colleagues' chagrin, fame and good fortune just seemed to follow her.

It was home-loving Judy who had always thought she would remain in Manchester, the bleak, rainy city where she was born and brought up. She'd had three years away when she went to Bristol University, a few months working in London, and a brief spell in Norwich, where she worked at Anglia Television. But she always went home. No one who knew Judy believed she would ever uproot herself and leave Manchester for good. Her children were settled in schools, she had one of the best jobs in television, her widowed mother Anne, in her eighties, lived close enough to visit every day if need be, and she had a home which, while not lavish, suited the ordinary way she wished to live. But the routine was becoming oppressive.

Then, early in 1995, it all started to change. Tom and Dan, Judy's eighteen-year-old twins by her first husband, David Henshaw, were studying for 'A' levels. They would be finished by the summer of 1996 and ready to move to London where they wanted to go to college. Chloe and Jack, Judy's children by Richard, would soon be ready to move to secondary school. If they were ever going to move, 1996 was the year to do it, before the children were due to settle into the last stage of their education.

Perhaps most importantly, Richard wanted to go home. Born in Romford, Essex, he hadn't lived in the south for nearly twenty years. Such a move would mean he could spend more time with his widowed mum and sister, Liz.

But family wasn't the only reason he wanted to leave his comfortable house in Old Broadway, Didsbury. The force that was driving him was stronger than homesickness. This was the logical next stage in a career that had been planned with military precision. And perhaps it was the stage where Richard Madeley would finally realise his dream.

It was because Judy understood the ambition that drove her

husband – his need for new and exciting challenges – that she was finally persuaded to take the leap into the unknown. For the love of her husband, and at a time in her career when she might otherwise have been thinking of slowing down, she was prepared to move her family and herself to a city where she knew no one and had no friends.

There are those who believe that the move to London could prove to be the downfall of Britain's golden couple.

'The trouble with Richard and Judy is they're too entrenched in what they do on daytime television,' says one TV executive who has worked with them over the past ten years. 'They had a crack at prime time when they did the *Richard and Judy Show*. But the trouble with them is that they have a very strong view of what they do and what they want. And they are not very good about taking direction about how what they do on daytime can be translated into what you do during prime time. Richard and Judy have been doing what they do on *This Morning* for so long that they find it difficult to change to the much faster pace of prime time. People have tried to coach them but it doesn't work.

'In fact, if you look at all the other shows they have done, apart from *This Morning*, none of them seem to have done terribly well. The view inside TV is that they are good at *This Morning* but forays into anything else have not been a runaway success.'

None of this seems to bother the public, who still seem fiercely loyal to this couple whose self-confessed 'ordinariness' has proved to be a strength rather than a weakness. They bark and bicker at each other on screen, they laugh, and they lay bare their secrets.

Having suffered problems with her weight, Judy has become a champion for the size-16-and-over woman. For another presenter, a series of unflattering pictures in a bikini, splashed all over the tabloid press, could have been professional poison. Yet for Judy Finnigan it only brought her a step closer to her adoring fans. They know what it is to have a less-than-perfect body. They too fail at every diet they attempt. Instead of alienating viewers, the change in her looks seems to have entrenched her more firmly in their hearts. Instead of berating her about her weight, instead of expecting her to conform to the blandly glamorous image of what we have all been conditioned to think a TV presenter should look like, the viewers empathise with Judy Finnigan. They know what she feels; how hard life can be sometimes.

Richard and Judy are undoubtedly stars, yet viewers believe this extraordinary couple to be 'ordinary', just like them, despite their earnings in excess of a million pounds a year. This ordinariness stems from the fact that they reveal their lives together on screen, something which has never before been done on television. Not even Anne and Nick, during their time at TV AM, engendered this kind of special empathy with their viewers.

In the past five years, with the exception of a spate of publicity surrounding their new chat show, *Richard and Judy Tonight*, the couple have steadfastly refused to give interviews to national newspapers on the basis that they value their privacy. Yet the illusion they create on screen is that they have no privacy, no secrets from the viewers. For people who are reluctant to reveal anything of themselves in an interview, they are amazingly frank about their lives on screen. They talk about their bills, their babies, their overdrafts, their illnesses, their fears – all the things the rest of us sitting at home talk about.

But the reality is that this couple don't have exactly the same worries as the rest of us. They are protected and cosseted by a TV company that is terrified that one day it might lose them. They earn more than almost any other presenter on television. They are not ordinary at all.

1 How It All Started

ICHARD AND JUDY, Judy and Richard – names that fit together as neatly as Fred and Ginger. Names so indelibly printed on the consciousness of Britain that it's hard to remember a time when they weren't there, when they weren't together. But Richard and Judy might never have been a couple – at least not on screen, not on *This Morning*. Britain's hottest TV couple could actually have been Richard and Jayne.

Today Jayne Irving presents UK Living's *Live at Three* magazine programme. But back in 1988 she was the popular host of TV AM's *After Nine* slot. It was in the summer of that year that Jayne received a phone call from Granada asking her to travel to Manchester for secret talks about the launch of a brand-new daytime TV show to be called *This Morning*.

Jayne wasn't sure at first. She already had a very good job at TV AM. It was high profile and paid big money, with a guaranteed audience of millions. It was a job she had worked long and hard to get and the attractive presenter didn't know whether she had the courage to gamble all that on a show that, within the industry, was already being dubbed a disaster waiting to happen. The inside gossip was that *This Morning* was doomed to failure, and although it *was* just gossip, it was enough to make Jayne Irving think twice about throwing in a job on a show that was the TV success story of the early-eighties. If *This Morning* turned out to be a failure then Jayne knew that, as one of the two main 'anchors', she would be seen as in some way responsible. That's how it is in television.

If a programme is a rip-roaring success, the presenter gets 'star treatment', with a star-size salary to match. If it fails, then never mind about the directors, the producers and the executives who are the brains behind the flop. The presenter takes the rap – at least so far as the viewers are concerned. And in television, what the viewers think counts.

If *This Morning* bombed then Jayne's career, her reputation, everything she had worked for, would be consigned to television's scrap heap. Conversely, she knew that if *This Morning* were a success, her career would go into overdrive. She would have money, power, and kudos within the industry for 'pulling it off'. She would be hailed as 'Queen of Daytime', and this male presenter she'd never heard of would be her king.

Jayne knew she had more experience than Richard Madeley, then still a relative unknown working in the regions. She'd been on the network more than two years now and was already a household name, which would automatically give her a huge advantage. It was certainly tempting.

The new show's format had already been explained to her at great length by Granada's entertainment boss, David Liddiment, the man who had first approached her. She had also been told about the pivotal role she would take – sharing the main stage with this man Richard Madeley whom Granada seemed so excited about. Jayne discovered later that Richard had always been first choice as the male presenter for *This Morning*. Right from the time Granada knew they were going to have to put together a pilot for a new morning magazine show, this polished young man was the person they wanted in an armchair adjacent to Jayne's.

So what was she to do? Should she listen to her own doubts about this unproven new show? Or should she take a leap into the unknown and accept the consequences, whatever they were?

Finally, after much cajoling by Granada executives, and even more soul-searching on her own part, Jayne decided that gambling on the success of *This Morning* was a risk worth taking. There were no guarantees in this world, but the chance to host her own show was just too tantalising to turn down. David Liddiment had offered her the job and was pressing her for a quick decision. Why not? She'd do it.

For better or for worse, Jayne Irving was going to be co-presenter of *This Morning*, and she realised that the idea was beginning to grow on her.

But unfortunately, as is often the case in the media merry-go-round, Jayne Irving was then told that she was no longer needed.

This was no reflection on her ability – merely another example of the insecurity and quickfire decision making within the television world. Choosing a presenter for a key job involves gaining the interest and enthusiasm of a great many executives. It only takes one to rock the boat.

The outcome was a blow for the able young presenter, not so much in career terms as she was already host of a successful network show. But she felt hugely disappointed, especially as, from the outset, *they* had pursued *her*. 'I know *This Morning* is something I would have enjoyed,' she has said to friends.

Everyone at Granada was surprised by the decision not to hire Jayne, especially as there were only a few days to go before filming started on the new pilot. Meanwhile Max Gressor, the man who had been asked to produce the pilot, was at home in Derbyshire when he heard the news that Jayne Irving was not being taken on. He had only days to find a woman to co-present the show with Richard Madeley.

Richard didn't know Jayne Irving personally. Naturally he was sorry that her feelings had been hurt, but he had never made any secret of the fact that he believed a husband-and-wife presenting team would be a ratings winner. He wanted Granada to give the female presenter's job to his wife of two years, Judy Finnigan.

'To give Richard credit, he never wavered in his belief that Judy would be absolutely right for *This Morning*,' reveals a close friend of theirs, who worked with them at Granada. 'Richard went into Steve Morrison's office, who was then head of regional programmes, to plead Judy's case. It was he who told Steve that the married couple thing was a great idea. He was very shrewd and saw the possibilities of a real-life Mr and Mrs.

'Sometimes people underestimated Richard. But he had good

ideas, and the idea to put him and Judy together was his. Yes, he wanted to work with her because she was his wife. But more than that, he realised that it was a brilliant concept, something that had never been done before.'

In the years after she'd landed it, Judy always said that the fact that she and Richard were married was nothing to do with her getting the job. But it was certainly one of the pivotal reasons why Granada finally gave in to pressure from Richard Madeley, adamant that a husband-and-wife team could win ratings.

'You could say that I just happened to be in the right place at the right time,' Judy has said. And there at least she is right. The right place was at Richard's side. The right time was when Granada finally recognised the truth of what he was saying.

But the new programme was not just to be confined to the regions: *This Morning* was going network, and in the eyes of many of those who mattered, Judy Finnigan did not at first seem to have the essential prerequisites. She wasn't the typically young, slim, glamorous girl that was the norm, but a woman of 40 with four children under the age of eleven.

Judy Finnigan had never been an ambitious woman – but then, she hadn't had to be. At first, success just seemed to follow her around. A combination of good looks, a sharp mind, and the fact that she always seemed to have the knack of being in the right place at the right time, had meant that her career flourished effortlessly. Jobs just fell into her lap. Fame, albeit regional, settled on her shoulders like some glowing mantle. But, by 1988, it seemed to many that she had gone as far as she was going.

Those male executives who, in Judy's early years at Granada, had seen so much promise in the young presenter, had long since gone. The new breed was unimpressed: 'As executives change, so does the received wisdom,' says a producer who was working in Manchester at the time. 'Judy was not doing anything particular in her career. It seemed to be going no-where.'

And so, as her job opportunities dried up, the lull in Judy's career had become common knowledge. Sometimes presenters were 'in', sometimes they were 'out'. In 1988, through no fault of her own, she was seen as out.

Says a lifelong friend of Judy's, who has also worked closely with her: 'At that time she was seen as someone who hadn't quite made her mark yet.'

One female producer who was working with Judy says: 'The truth was that at that time Judy just was not considered to be network.'

Richard Madeley, on the other hand, very definitely *was* network. He had always been first choice for *This Morning* by bosses who recognised this suave, well-groomed, good-looking young man as 'star' material.

But it wasn't only his looks that impressed them. He was polished, had a relaxed presenting style, but more importantly had the ability to stay cool in a crisis. This was exactly the kind of man they needed to produce 90 minutes of live television every day. What kind of woman would complement Richard's self-possession, charm and warmth? What woman would help him generate the 'magic' that would be a ratings grabber and create a hit show?

In Richard Madeley's mind there was never any question as to who that woman should be. He wanted the woman he loved to be sitting alongside him in that Liverpool studio. He just knew Judy was right for the job, and nothing anyone could say to him would make him think differently.

It wasn't just out of loyalty he wanted her to be his co-presenter. He'd presented *Granada Reports* with her four or five years previously and knew they were good together. They'd also recreated the old magic in Granada's first Telethon in 1988.

Says Jim Walker who was the producer of Judy's show *Scramble*: 'Richard and Judy did the Telethon two years running and they were brilliant. Terribly professional. They did 27 hours straight off the belt. It took some stamina.'

As well as having total confidence in her ability to carry off *This Morning*, Richard also wanted his wife to be part of a show he believed in his heart was going to be one of TV's great success stories. He had a gut feeling that he and Judy would be perfect to take Granada's flagship show into the ratings battle.

What he didn't know was that at the time Jayne Irving wasn't the only candidate being considered for the post.

A dark-haired young Scottish reporter called Sheena McDonald had caught the eye of head of regionals, Steve Morrison. Sheena, who now presents Channel 4's *House to House* and has carved herself a reputation as one of this country's most formidable heavyweight political interviewers, was working as a local programmes presenter on Scottish television. She was bright, she was feisty and she was attractive. Sheena was approached about the possibility of presenting *This Morning*.

But even though she was young, her inclination was towards more 'serious' television. She felt that a magazine programme was not the direction in which she wanted to take her career. 'I don't want to talk about jobs I didn't do,' she said recently. But the fact was, although grateful for Morrison's confidence in her, the Richard and Sheena show was not what she wanted.

In some quarters of Granada it came as a relief to those who believed Sheena was 'too posh' and too intellectually weighty to front the frothy, glitzy daytime show which had taken root in the minds of a handful of TV's top executives a few months before.

At this point, Granada were already way behind schedule in making their pilot. The other companies who were bidding for the 90-minute slot had started planning as far back as May. Granada were the last into the ring. With just a week to go, Richard was told that his wife would be allowed to partner him in the pilot that would be shown to the Daytime Committee. The feeling at Granada was that, if they were given the commission to make *This Morning*, they could fiddle about with the female presenter and format later. All that mattered now was making the pilot.

It should have been good news for the Madeleys. And it was – at least for Richard. He was ecstatic when he heard his wife was going to be able to work alongside him. He had been happy since the day he'd been told he was going to be the male anchor on *This Morning*. Richard wasn't worried about the fact that it was a new concept. As far as he was concerned, it was a big chance. He refused to listen to those people who said he might fail. 'Failure' wasn't a word in his vocabulary. Nor was he daunted by the prospect of the grind of doing 90 minutes of live network television every day. He relished the idea. It was what he had been waiting for.

But for his wife it was different. 'Judy freaked out when she heard she was being given the pilot,' says a friend. 'Not only was this going to be the biggest test of her career. *This Morning*, if it happened, was going to be live and it was going to be network and both these things made Judy very nervous. She knew she needed *This Morning* but she was scared of it. While Richard savoured the prospect of the fame, Judy's reaction to it was vastly more complicated.'

But, however nervous she was and however frightening she found it, Judy knew she had to pull herself together – not just for her career but for Richard's. He had tried so hard to make this pilot happen for them. She couldn't let him down.

The following weekend the pilot was put together in Liverpool. Everyone working on the show knew the brief. It had to be glitzy and glamorous but practical as well – a women's magazine transferred to the small screen. But it also had to contain the adult educational requirement of the IBA (the Independent Broadcasting Authority). The idea was that the adult educational material, which until then had been dry and totally unappetising, would be transformed into easily assimilable little strands which would then be woven into the main body of the programme. No one would realise that while they watched they were also being educated.

By Sunday evening the pilot was finally finished. Everyone involved in it knew it was good. In fact, it was *very* good considering the time they'd had to put it together. Max Gressor was happy. The Richard and Judy pairing had worked brilliantly. But would it be brilliant enough to win over the Daytime Committee?

Since the astonishing success of *This Morning*, many people have laid claim to the kudos of creating it. But the truth is that it was born from an idea seeded within a group of TV's most powerful executives.

The Daytime Committee was set up in 1988 when ITV reviewed the whole process of commissioning for the network. Before that ITV had a 'licence to print money' with programmes being commissioned on the 'smoke-filled room' principle by just a handful of powerful men, notably Lord Grade and Sidney Bernstein. Ratings mattered less than politics in those days because ratings were pretty much guaranteed in this monopoly situation. Then came the 'Flexipool' idea, when ideas from everyone across the network went into a pool and were selected, or not, by a series of committees made up from TV executives. There was a Children's Committee, a Factual Committee, a Drama Committee, and there was the Daytime Committee. It was this committee that was responsible for commissioning *This Morning*.

Lis Howell, now director of programming for Sky's UK Living, was head of news at Border Television in Carlisle when she was invited to be a member of one of the new committees that would decide what would appear on our screens.

'Everyone hated the reorganisation within ITV. But it was great for people like me because committees were set up to judge the programmes and what was happening to them. I suddenly found myself on the Daytime Committee, part of whose job it was to reorganise ITV mornings.'

The Daytime Committee met every month at the headquarters of the ITV Association in Mortimer Street. The chairman was Alan Boyd, programme controller of TVS and a former head of light entertainment at LWT. Committee members included Tim Riordan of Thames, later director of programming on Sky One, Rod Caird from Granada who went on to work for an independent production company, Graham Ironside from Yorkshire, Derek Clark from HTV, and Andy Allan from Central TV, later Carlton's director of programmes.

'These were great big men with great big egos,' says Lis Howell. 'And I had to fight tooth and nail to get my views across.' But she knew she couldn't allow male prejudice to get in the way. There was work to be done and one of the priorities was to reorganise ITV mornings, which at that time was a ratings desert.

For years, mornings on ITV had been monstrously dull, an unappetising mix of adult educational programmes, which the ITV network was committed to running under the terms of the old Broadcasting Act. It was a worthy commitment but a doomed one. No one was actually watching ITV in the mornings, save for a handful of people who enjoyed crackly old black and white history films.

The afternoons boasted some decent shows for women. There were chat shows, cookery programmes, and a fair sprinkling of celebrity interviews. But the mornings stayed a barren affair, something which Lis Howell had discovered at first hand when she was on maternity leave looking after her baby, Alex.

'For the first time in my working life I was at home during the day and I saw the kind of garbage that was going out in the mornings. It was awful. Dry old educational programmes that were taking up good TV time. It was time that could be put to better use.'

Lis saw that the Daytime Committee knew it had to maintain its commitment to adult education: 'But our idea was to make it part of a magazine-type morning show.' And so the idea for *This Morning* was born.

Once the idea had been formulated, various ITV regions were asked to pitch for the 90-minute slot which would be made vacant in the daytime schedule.

'There were four companies who submitted a pilot show,' says Lis. 'There was one from Yorkshire, and one from Central TV in Birmingham. There was an extremely good one from Fern Britton and Andy Craig who were working for TVS at the time.' And there was Granada's.

'We whittled it down to two,' remembers Lis. 'The decision was between TVS and Granada.'

Finally the day arrived when the Daytime Committee had to decide which of the two programmes was to be awarded the slot. Would it be Granada, with its glamorous husband-and-wife presenting team, or would be be the upbeat TVS show? A lot rested on the committee's decision. Ninety minutes of live television was a huge prize for any television company. It was a prize that could generate millions of pounds in advertising revenue, providing the show was good, and a big steady commission like *This Morning* could stop a TV company having to lay off a lot of people. At that time many of the TV stations had huge staffs and high overheads, and with the advent of new technology into the industry many jobs would inevitably be shed. Landing the commission for a show like *This Morning* could keep masses of people in work. It could also boost the daily ratings schedule, which at that time was getting no help at all from ITV mornings.

On the creative side, a morning magazine programme would be breaking new ground, and if it was a success the company responsible for it would be lauded within the industry.

Because of everything that rested on the committee's decision, there had been much behind-the-scenes jockeying by the companies on the shortlist in an effort to clinch the prize. Members found themselves being wined and dined almost to the point of exhaustion by television executives determined to convince them that 'their' magazine show had the winning formula.

Lis Howell walked into Knighton House, offices of the ITV Association, on the day the committee was finally to decide who would get the commission to launch ITV into daytime television. 'If I'm honest, I was biased against Granada when going into the meeting that day,' says Lis. 'I was very pro-TVS because I liked Andy Craig and had worked with him before.

'But the truth was, when I sat down and watched those pilots again, *This Morning* was far and away the better show. I knew in my heart which programme had to get my vote. In fact, I remember the *This Morning* video to this day.

'It was filmed outside the studio, which was unusual in those days. And I'll never forget, they did this item which involved Richard and Judy walking along the dock. The item was about children swimming and they were filming the introduction to it with one of their own kids.

'Suddenly, and it obviously wasn't planed, the child ran

towards the edge of the dock. I can't remember whether it was Richard or Judy but one of them shot forward and grabbed the child before it had time to fall in.

'It was a reflex action, totally natural, the kind of thing any parent would have done. Back in 1988 it was the sort of thing that would have been edited out of a film. It would have been seen as a mistake. Remember, this was before the dawn of the *Big Breakfast* and we'd never had anything spontaneous like that on television before. I was impressed by that clip because I had a toddler of my own and I remember thinking that Richard and Judy did exactly what I would have done. It was that element, which had probably been a mistake, that finally turned me around in favour of Granada.'

Although Lis was by then totally convinced Granada should get the slot, there were still some members of the committee who were not so sure. Some were still firmly in favour of TVS's show. There was much heated discussion until finally Central TV's Andy Allan came out firmly in favour of the Granada pilot because of the husband-and-wife presenting team, saying it was a novel idea which many people would identify with.

Everyone realised he was right and so Granada won the most coveted prize in daytime television. The *This Morning* dream was about to become reality.

The commission was awarded just a few weeks before the show was due to go out on air. The news was the cause of much celebration and reinforced Granada's opinion that: 'If anyone can do it, we can.' But although everyone at Granada was delighted to get the commission, there was surprise in other areas of the TV industry that they had pulled it off, albeit by the skin of their teeth. People from other companies were upset, asking why, when Granada had come so late into the ring, they could walk away with the prize. Many people felt that the Manchester-based company was not the natural home for the slot. A morning magazine-type show was not seen to be their style of broadcasting.

But there was one woman with the talent to make *This Morning* into Granada's style of broadcasting – the same woman who invented the 'cosy' factor and injected it into a show that started with no money and no celebrities in a group of dank buildings in the heart of Liverpool's Albert Dock.

Dianne Nelmes was a producer at the BBC's *Brass Tacks* programme in Manchester when she was asked to meet David Liddiment at Granada to discuss a new programme. In itself that was unusual. Granada didn't take lightly the defection of talented people from their organisation, and Dianne Nelmes had done exactly that the previous year when she resigned her job as a senior researcher on Granada's flagship current affairs programme, *World in Action*. Despite working on some of the most highly rated shows, she could see no prospect of promotion to producer, and so she left.

Her populist programmes, which investigated tranquilliser addiction, slimming, the NHS and old people's homes, were unpopular with some of the programme's so-called 'serious' journalists, who saw them as out of step with *World in Action*'s heavyweight image. Or at least they thought that until the ratings came in and they saw that Nelmes's mass-appeal programmes were consistently near the top. But, despite her success, Dianne was told she was too young at present for a producer's job. She didn't want to wait and when BBC's *Brass Tacks* stepped in and offered her a producer's job, she grabbed it with both hands. Dianne had been at *Brass Tacks* less than a year when the call came from David Liddiment. They were making a new magazine programme. Was she interested in being the editor?

Dianne had never been hidebound by what was perceived as 'serious' television. Many journalists would have been reluctant to leave the rarefied atmosphere of current affairs for the world of cookery slots and celebrity interviews. But not Dianne Nelmes. Even today she remains one of the few executives in British television who could edit *Panorama* as successfully as she could *This Morning*, because she instinctively understands both disciplines.

Lindsay Charlton, who was a reporter on *Granada Reports* in Manchester when Dianne was news editor, and is now a presenter at LWT, says: 'Dianne is a rare and valuable commodity in British television. She can work in the heavy current affairs medium or the light entertainment medium. Many people who work for *Panorama* would think a programme like *This Morning* was beneath them. Dianne doesn't see it like that. To her they are different programmes with a different agenda. But she doesn't see one as better than the other.'

The appointment of Dianne Nelmes as editor of *This Morning* came as a surprise to many. Max Gressor, who had been responsible for the successful pilot, was offered the role of deputy editor.

With just three weeks to go before the show was due to go on air, the team was finally in place. But still no one had the vaguest idea how they were going to fill 90 minutes of live television five days a week. There was already a basic shape to the programme, a broad outline that had been established in the pilot. But until Dianne arrived none of the ideas or concepts could be fleshed out.

Three weeks before the first-ever *This Morning* went on air, a team of producers, directors and technicians arrived en masse at the Albert Dock. What they saw filled them with horror. Because there was nothing – no offices, no phones, no typewriters, no studio. Everything had to be built from scratch in those old warehouses, some of which had been empty for years. The only person to have an office was one of Granada's general managers and so everyone squatted in his space.

There were still no films or stories in the can; there was no stockpile of items in case anything went wrong. Apart from Richard and Judy, none of the presenters had even been found, let alone signed. It was chaos. One of the producers who was there in the early days says: 'Dianne hadn't arrived at this stage and no one knew what they were supposed to be doing. So a group of us went to the nearest newsagent's and bought every women's magazine we could find. We nearly collapsed under the weight of them but finally we got them back to the studio and raided them for ideas.'

Then there were the presenters to sort out. The only person they knew for sure was coming was Fred Talbot, the weatherman, who has since become famous for his flying leaps across *This Morning*'s floating weather map. Fred was Granada TV's first-ever weatherman, broadcasting five times a day through-out the north-west, though he started his life in television as a presenter of science shows. Fred had been featured in the original pilot and so far was the only ancillary presenter who was a dead cert.

Denise Robertson was already an agony aunt working on Tyneside when she was approached by Dianne Nelmes. Four years before, in 1984, when the last of her five children had gone to university, Denise had finally got down to writing her first novel, *The Land of Lost Content*, which won her the Constable Fiction Trophy and became a bestseller. She had begun writing stories for women's magazines in 1970 after her first husband, Alex, died of cancer. Until then the 37-year-old widow had been dabbling with literary pieces that paid a pittance. After Alex died Denise knew she had to find a way to support their son and so she asked her agent what she could write that paid weekly. The answer was popular short fiction and she carried on writing even after she met and married her second husband, Jack, in 1972.

Dianne had met Denise in the north-east when she was a reporter on the BBC's *Look North* programme. The two had liked each other instantly and became friends. Denise was the obvious choice when Dianne found herself searching for an agony aunt for *This Morning*.

So, they had their weatherman and their agony aunt. Now the hunt was on for a likeable, sympathetic GP, the type of man with whom people would feel at ease while talking about their ailments. Richard and Judy pitched in on this one. Chris Steele was their family GP in Manchester. He was a gentle, softly spoken Geordie, the kind of man who had the ability to make people feel relaxed, and was also able to give practical help and reassurance at the same time. He was still very much a hands-on GP, working in a busy practice with 18,000 patients on its list. Chris's forte was, and is, helping people give up their addiction to nicotine, a speciality which has come in very handy over the years as he has helped dozens of *This Morning* guests to kick the habit.

Ten days before the show was due to go on air, they still

hadn't found a cook. Years before, Susan Brookes had been thrown out of cookery classes at school – for talking. It was hardly an auspicious start for a woman who was later to become one of the most famous cooks in Britain. Susan had trained as a teacher, writing features for the local newspaper in her spare time. She had gone to live in the picturesque village of Giggleswick in North Yorkshire, the village that boasted Russell Harty as a resident, after her husband Warwick Brookes took the job of housemaster at Giggleswick School.

In 1980 Susan landed a job as researcher at Granada. She worked on the nightly news programme, *Granada Reports*, and later on the *Krypton Factor*, before moving in front of the cameras to co-present a programme called *Late Night From Two* with Shelley Rhode. It was the suggestion that all food programmes on television were 'too posh' that led to the launch of Susan's cookery career in a programme called *On the Market*. She was signed for *This Morning* just a week before it went on air.

Dianne didn't have to go far to find Andrew and Liz Collinge, *This Morning*'s hair and make-up experts. Andrew had trained at Michaeljohn in London but was running a family hairdressing business on Merseyside.

The last signing was wine expert Charles Metcalfe, who was contracted with less than seven days to go.

The on-screen team was finally in place but still it was touch and go whether the studio would be ready in time. Everything had to be built from scratch and even with gangs of workmen and technicians at it round the clock, no one could be sure it would all be ready for the Big Day. In those last few days before transmission, researchers and producers were turning up at the Albert Dock at 7am and not leaving until past midnight.

'We didn't sleep, we didn't eat. But still it was wonderful to be there,' says a producer who was in on it at the beginning. 'It was new, it was fun, even if the only thing that kept us rocketing along was the adrenaline which came from the fear that it was all going to go wrong.

'It was fantastic to be in on the ground floor of something

record-breaking like that. We were carving out something that was totally new, rather than just fine-tuning or maintaining something that was already there. And, in television, that's as good as it gets.'

With just 24 hours to go, Richard and Judy, together with all the other presenters and technical staff, did a dry run of the show. There was no time to do any more.

Richard and Judy were nervous but they were as ready as they'd ever be. Judy, in particular, looked fantastic. Her Achilles' heel had always been her weight, but from the moment she discovered that Granada were sticking with the husband-and-wife presenting team, she went on the biggest crash diet of her life.

'She transformed herself,' says one of the reporters in the Granada newsroom at the time. 'She ate nothing but Lean Cuisines in the lead-up to the launch of *This Morning*. Richard was doing everything he could to support her and the joke in the office was that the two of them would go home, get a glass of wine, take a Lean Cuisine out of the deep freeze and settle down for the evening. But whatever she did, you just couldn't believe this was the same girl. She lost stones. The woman absolutely made herself over. She had new hair, new suits, everything. And so by the time she was ready to go on air she looked better than she ever had.'

D-Day finally arrived. Most of the technical staff had been working through the previous night, ironing out the last few wrinkles. Producers and researchers worked alongside them, doing everything they could to make sure the show went off without a hitch. The atmosphere in the studio was electric. Shouts of 'Good luck' and 'Break a leg' rang out as everyone took their places in readiness for the cue that would tell them they were on air. With frantic hand signals, the floor manager counted Richard and Judy into the programme: 'Five, four, three, two, one . . .'

At precisely 10.40am on Monday, 3 October 1988, the *This Morning* theme tune was broadcast into homes all over Britain.

'Hello, I'm Richard Madeley . . .'

'. . . and I'm Judy Finnigan.'

And a TV legend was born.

The first hurdle was the phone-in. Richard and Judy were asking people to call in with their views on whether a woman should have a career or stay at home. But no one at *This Morning*'s offices could be sure that anyone would actually be watching, let alone take the trouble to ring. The terror was almost tangible.

They needn't have worried. Within twenty minutes there were more than 500 calls. The switchboard was jammed.

The 90-minute show went almost without a hitch and before the credits finished rolling, the champagne corks were popping. There was still a lot to be done, everyone knew that. But for one-and-a-half-hours, against all the odds, a small but deliriously happy *This Morning* team had delivered a programme that didn't just fill up a black hole in our screens – they'd filled it with a programme that was about to make TV history.

2 Judy

JUDY FINNIGAN HAD ALWAYS wielded an extraordinary power over the opposite sex. Men would become her willing slaves. The intoxicating mixture of her innate and obvious sexuality, intelligence and vulnerability coupled with her professional strength captivated any man who was exposed to it. It was a power that mystified women who could not understand why this far from svelte woman seemed to have every man she met at her beck and call.

It led one of the women who worked at *Granada Reports* where Judy was a presenter to say, 'God knows what she's got. But if you could bottle it, you'd make a fortune.'

Men had always understood exactly what it was that Judy Finnigan had. They didn't see her as fat – they saw her as delightfully curvaceous. They didn't see bad dress sense – they saw a woman who knew how best to show off her assets. They didn't see the *femme fatale* that other women saw, but rather a woman who understood her own sexuality yet needed to have it reinforced by their attention.

'She loved the company of men,' says one of the reporters at Granada at the time. 'She was a very sexy lady who exuded sensuality and enjoyed flirting. Women don't get it, I know, but Judy has that wonderful mix of maternalism and sexuality which you don't normally get in one package.'

Female associates could hardly fail to notice the effect she had on men. 'Judy is a very sexual woman,' says a woman producer who worked with her on *Granada Reports*. 'I remember once watching her in the Stables Bar where we all used to drink after work and in the end I had to look away, because that kind of naked sexuality made me feel a bit inferior as a woman. But she had an incredible effect on men. They'd be looking at her with their tongues hanging out.'

Judy was born on 16 May 1948 at North Manchester Maternity Home, slap-bang in the middle of a baby boom. Just three days before she was born, the registrar general published his report showing that Britain's birth rate was up a staggering 21 per cent on the previous year. John and Anne Finnigan didn't hold much with statistics – after four hard years of war, the only news they were interested in was good news, and in the month before their baby daughter was born, the good news was that twelve extra clothing coupons were to be made available to everyone. It was just what they needed to kit their baby out.

Judy's recollections of her childhood are happy ones. 'I had a typical *Coronation Street* working-class Manchester upbringing,' she says. 'I remember every year as a child I would go on the Whitsuntide Walks – the big attraction for me being I could wear a long white frock down to my gollies. All the children used to walk through the streets of Manchester and our reward afterwards was a glass of cold milk and an iced bun.'

Her childhood was like any other spent growing up in those tough post-war years. Her father was working, there was always food on the table, and while they didn't have everything they needed, they were happy. But then, when she was five years old, Judy developed measles which was to trigger a heart condition that is with her to this day.

'I was so ill on my fifth birthday I couldn't go upstairs,' Judy remembers. 'It's a very working-class thing that when you are seriously ill they bring you downstairs to lie in the front room. It usually means you are at death's door, which is why so many working-class people have this thing, no matter how ill they are, about going upstairs to bed.'

Measles left no visible scar but the heart murmur remains.

Judy was a bookish child. She enjoyed school and especially reading. She was always near the top of her class which was why, when she was eleven years old, she was invited to sit the entrance exam for the exclusive Manchester High School. In the late-fifties, the fee-paying Manchester High had a high

Oxbridge success rate and was steeped in weighty academic tradition.

The school had been devastated by enemy bombs in 1940, but not even the Germans could destroy the spirit of a centre of learning founded by a group of Manchester women who 'wished to provide for Manchester's daughters what had been provided without stint for Manchester's sons'.

The pupils of Manchester High were generally regarded as the *crème de la crème*, a notion promoted by both teachers and pupils alike. They were either rich or clever or both. These young ladies were not just expected to perform well in exams – they were expected to go on to be high achievers in life, to have careers, to go out into the world as doctors, lawyers, academics . . . why not even prime minister? Here was a school that had risen out of the revolutionary fire of the Suffragette Movement. Its founders were pioneers of women's education. Much was expected of those lucky enough to pass through its hallowed portals.

On the morning Judy was due to sit her scholarship entrance exam, John and Anne Finnigan hugged their daughter and wished her good luck as she set off on the short walk to the school. They had prospered in the years since Judy was born, and their improved circumstances had enabled them to buy a large post-war semi in Birchfields Road, Fallowfield.

The front of the house, with its wide bay windows and arched doorway, looked out on to the busy main road, and at the back its long narrow garden ended where the hockey pitch and the lush green playing fields of Manchester High began. Set slightly back from the road, the concrete driveway was big enough to hold two cars. But back in 1959, John and Anne Finnigan didn't have to worry about fleets of cars.

In the eleven years since Judy had been born, John and Anne had had another child, a son called Roger who eventually became as obsessed with Manchester United as his elder brother Cal. But even though things were going well, money was tight and no matter how they did their sums, no matter how many economies they made, they would still never be able to afford the fees for Manchester High School. They desperately wanted Judy to do well, but if she failed to win a scholarship they were in trouble. They knew she was bright. They were about to find out just how bright.

On that spring morning in 1959, as Judy skipped off to sit the exam that could change the course of her life for ever, John and Anne Finnigan knew it was out of their hands.

Judy had been nervous as she walked past the cold, unwelcoming walls of a school that could, if she passed the scholarship exam, be the place where she would spend the next seven years of her life. And as she walked through the school's well-tended gardens and into the main reception which looked out on to the science labs beyond, she knew this was where she wanted to be. Sitting in a never-ending corridor, with its high ceilings and floors polished to look like glass, Judy was terrified. She knew how important this exam was and was shaking with nerves as she sat waiting with the other entrants.

At eleven years old, Judy was already dazzlingly pretty. Her blonde hair, shining and freshly washed, had twisted itself into a mass of springy curls. She was chubby, though not excessively so. But the striking thing about this girl, whose body was still caught on the cusp between childhood and womanhood, was her face. At an age when most girls' faces are still undefined, Judy's was already beautiful.

She sat the scholarship exam and a few weeks later her parents were ecstatic when they were told their daughter had passed with flying colours. Judy Finnigan had taken the first step away from her humble background. From now on she would be groomed as one of the 'young ladies' of Manchester High.

She started in September of that year. The weeks before had been a frantic and expensive spending spree. Though there would be no fees to pay, thanks to the scholarship, there had been much to buy. The school's striking black and gold uniform wasn't cheap. There was the black gabardine trench coat, the black blazer trimmed with sparkling gold braid, the black gabardine skirt and the cream shirt. For summer there were dresses in red, yellow or blue gingham check. One girl was sent home that first week because she didn't have a pair of indoor shoes. To Judy and all the other scholarship girls this was a revelation. Where she came from, you had one pair and you wore them indoors and outdoors. And then there was the beret. Oh, how she hated that beret!

It was an exciting, frightening, uncertain time. Everything was so different here. It took a while for the scholarship girls to settle in. They felt out of place in this rather grand school. All the other girls were the self-possessed offspring of the rich who were determined that their daughters should receive the best education money could buy. They had beautiful clothes, beautiful homes, beautiful lives – and took their privileged lives for granted. They had the kind of affluent existence that Judy and the other scholarship girls had only read about in books. There was a lot of adjusting to do, and some of it was hard.

It wasn't that anyone teased the scholarship girls or tried to make them feel out of place. It was just that they *did*. The school, with its grand portico and polished floors, was like nothing they had ever seen before. For the first time in their lives these girls from the back streets of Manchester were being made to confront wealth, privilege and learning at the highest level. This was a whole new world, one where they did not as yet belong – though one day, if they were lucky, they might.

Says one of the girls who was in Judy's crowd: 'We always felt a bit apart somehow. It wasn't that anyone made us feel like that. It was just something inside us. Something working class.'

Judy had barely been at the school a month when she was told by her teachers that her Mancunian accent would have to go. Soft and barely discernible as it was, it was strong enough to offend the genteel ears of the mistresses of Manchester High. Judy was told she would have to have elocution lessons, which would be provided by the school, until all traces of her accent had been eradicated.

But while the teachers may have stamped out her accent, they weren't up to crushing her spirit: 'She was tremendous fun to be around,' says one of Judy's closest friends at school, Clarissa Hyman. 'She was lively, bright, intelligent. She was wonderful company. Judy would always be the one to say the wittiest things. Her views on things mattered. Everyone wanted to know what she thought. There are lots of groups and gangs in school, and for every one of those groups there is a leader. Judy was our leader. She was the one who set the agenda. She set the tone of what was happening. I suppose, in a way, she told us what we should be thinking about certain things. If she said something was naff, then mostly we agreed with her. She wasn't bossy or anything like that. She did it by force of her personality. Most of us listened to her because, I suppose, we wanted to be like her.'

While Judy Finnigan could never quite let herself forget that she was a scholarship girl, she soon learned to throw herself into school life with gusto. The teachers were all rather forbidding but somehow, with her sharp mind and ready smile, Judy always managed to keep on their right side.

'The teachers were terribly strict,' remembers one of the school's old girls. 'It wasn't that they hit you, although there were one or two who would rap your knuckles with a cane. Their approach was more psychological than physical. They could wither you with a glance.

'We had a Latin teacher called Miss Rouff who used to have two little plaits of hair wound round her ears. She wore flat sandals and was like some terrifying Valkyrie. She was a formidable woman.'

But, as Judy discovered, if your grades were good and you did your work, then you could keep the wrath of the teachers at bay.

Judy was fifteen when she discovered boys and the Beatles. The Fab Four had sprung to fame just 40 miles away in the Cavern in Liverpool, and Judy Finnigan was one of their greatest fans. So much so that when word got out that they were going to be playing at the Odeon in Manchester, Judy and her friend Clarissa persuaded their parents to let them queue up all night to buy tickets. 'It was seen as a terribly adventurous thing to do,' remembers Clarissa. 'We took our sleeping bags and then when it got cold my dad arrived with a Thermos flask and some sandwiches.

'Judy always liked John Lennon the best. We all suspected it was because he had intellectual pretensions.'

Although Judy enjoyed school life, there was one aspect of it that filled her with dread: games lessons.

Says Clarissa: 'We avoided gym like the plague. In fact we always made sure we had period pains four weeks out of every month.'

Clarissa says that when she and Judy were actually forced out on to the hockey pitch on cold winter days, they would wait until the teacher wasn't looking then make a dash for the fence that separated Judy's back garden from the school playing fields. 'For years we hid out in Judy's bedroom playing records and drinking coffee while everyone else was running round like mad things outside. No one ever discovered our little ruse.'

When Judy was sixteen, the sixties were in full swing and the style quake shook Manchester High to its foundations. It seemed as if the whole world was in flux. Men were flying to the moon. Attitudes and events were changing with bewildering rapidity. Girls were taking the revolutionary contraceptive pill, which meant they could have sex just for fun. There were important social and political innovations, not to mention a musical revolution. It was one of the great transitional periods of this century and the yong Judy Finnigan was slap-bang in the middle of it.

Tamla Motown had exploded on to the music scene. The Rolling Stones were screaming that they couldn't Get No Satisfaction – and there was a fashion crisis going on in the fifth-form common room of Manchester High.

Suddenly the black gabardine skirts that had lain comfortably on the knee for as long as anyone could remember were hitched up to near indecency. The girls all blacked their eyes with lashings of mascara and smothered their lips with death-pale pink lipstick. But it was their hair that posed the biggest problems. Or at least, not their hair but the dreaded berets. The teachers were sticklers for insisting they must be worn at all times when the girls were outside the school gates. But, with impossibly high beehive hairstyles, there was never anywhere to put them. 'We stuck them on to the back of our heads with kirby grips,' recalls one former pupil. 'You couldn't see from the front whether we had them on or not and that suited us just fine.'

But it wasn't just make-up and music that were proving big distractions – it was boys as well. The young Judy found herself dreamily preoccupied with the blond good looks of Justin Hayward, lead singer with the Moody Blues, but before long there were other young men on the horizon who proved to be more accessible.

'In the teachers' eyes the biggest crime you could commit at Manchester High was to be caught talking to a boy from Manchester Grammar School,' says an old school friend of Judy's. 'They were pond life as far as the teachers were concerned. In fact, all boys were pond life according to them. We were very segregated in those days – so segregated that we used to get hysterical when we were in the company of men. I remember there was a male Russian teacher who used to come into the school to teach us. We could not stop giggling whenever we were in a room with him and we all used to have these amazing fantasies about him.

'The only other man we ever had dealings with on a daily basis was the caretaker but none of us ever managed to conjure up a fantasy about *him*.'

It was about the time when Judy discovered she liked other boys that she made an exciting discovery – the feeling was mutual. Because of her approaching 'O' Levels she needed a quiet place to study and much of Judy's time after school was spent in the quiet of Manchester Central Library. Every day the girls in her clique would turn up at the library, skirts hitched up around their waists, berets perched precariously on the back of their beehives. Here they worked long and hard, because they knew that as soon as the study period was over, they could quite justifiably head straight off to the library's coffee bar. This wasn't so much a place to buy coffee, as a place for the girls of Manchester High to hang out with the boys from Manchester Grammar.

'We were all terribly pretentious,' says one of the girls from Judy's study group. 'We sat around all day drinking black coffee and talking about foreign films. We wore black clothes, black mascara, and thought we knew about everything. We were all horribly brainy and felt we were the source of Manchester's intellectual life. We'd sit around and talk about boys and *Hamlet* in the same breath. We were intellectual snobs. But then, that's what being at Manchester High was all about.'

It was in that coffee bar that Judy Finnigan first became aware that boys wanted to be around her as much as she wanted to be around them. They were fascinated by her brightness, her prettiness. And, yes, her sexiness.

'Judy always had a boyfriend,' remembers another of her old school friends. 'She was never ever alone after she discovered that boys liked her.'

While she was still at school she met a boy called John who, very soon after meeting her, asked her to marry him. John was a couple of years older than Judy when he met her, though still at school. Judy fell hopelessly in love for the first time. John was tall, fair haired and very good-looking, and all her friends fancied him like mad. But it was Judy he wanted.

She later said of him: 'We went out for three years and got engaged when I was nineteen. We broke up a year later and it was terrible. I had a holiday job checking the "A" Level results at Manchester University and every day when I went into the canteen they'd be playing "Knights In White Satin" by the Moody Blues and I would break down in tears.'

Says Judy's friend Clarissa: 'At that time Judy was one of the most attractive personalities I knew. I always knew she had certain qualities but no one ever dreamed she would go as far as she has.

'None of us was particularly ambitious in career terms. We all had ambitions in terms of exams but this was the sixties. We didn't feel we had to be worried or competitive about a career because we were all arrogant eough to assume we could do anything we wanted.'

There was no question of Judy thinking in terms of a career in television at the time. The whole world of TV was still the dark side of the moon as far as Judy's crowd was concerned. And in those days there was no such thing as a tabloid celebrity. It was a phenomenon that didn't exist – and if it had, it wouldn't have been quite the thing for a young lady from Manchester High.

Judy wasn't sure what she wanted to do when she left school. She thought she might try journalism. Her brother Cal was a journalist and he seemed to have a good life. But first she wanted to go to university to study English and drama. Armed with nine 'O' Levels and three 'A' Levels she had her pick, but the only course she was interested in doing was at Bristol. It had a very good reputation and was one of the few universities that offered a combined English and drama course.

Competition for places was fierce, but once again Judy's intelligence and promise took her exactly where she wanted to go. Her choice of course showed a burgeoning interest in a career based on performance, on pleasing an audience. She proved to be as successful in Bristol as she would later be on TV and graduated with honours. After a brief spell working in London, she returned to Manchester to decide what she was going to do with the rest of her life. Her engagement to John hadn't worked out but her three years away from home had taught her they'd been way too young even to have contemplated marriage at that stage.

In her early twenties Judy began working for Granada as a 'call girl'. Call girls and boys were employed by the company to be glorified 'go-fers'. They were usually university graduates whose job it was to guide actors and visitors who weren't familiar with the building to the part of it where they were working. The call girls and boys were all bright young things whose eventual ambition was to work in television, and they were employed by Granada in the expectation that they would stay with the company and eventually move to either editorial or production jobs.

In 1971 Judy landed a job as researcher on a programme called *Newsday* and soon after that she met and fell in love with her first husband, David Henshaw. At the time David was working for a regional show called *Six O One*, and Judy had spotted him one day while she was dashing round the building. She was instantly attracted to this shy, bookish, rather plump man who appeared to have all the qualities she was looking for. He was bright, sensitive, and committed to the same issues as she was. David was a serious academic journalist with strong socialist ideals. He was also a very gentle man and Judy wanted to get to know him better. But he was shy – not at all the type to pursue a startlingly pretty blonde like Judy Finnigan. But then he didn't have to, because Judy did all the running.

'She wanted him because he was a genuinely nice man. Everyone liked David,' says Irene McGlashin, one of Judy's best friends at Granada at the time.

After that, it didn't take very long for David Henshaw to fall in love with Judy. 'That's the amazing thing about her,' says another friend. 'No matter which bloke she ended up going out with, no matter how macho or strong they were when they met her, they always ended up being her slave. She went out with David because he was a nice bloke but he ended up running after her like all the others. He was quite plump at the time. He had at one time been very fat. I don't think he could ever quite believe that any woman could fancy him – especially a woman like Judy.'

Says another old friend: 'All Judy's men used to run after her making a fuss. Men were always fetching and carrying for Judy.'

They were married on 23 March 1974 at Manchester Register Office. Even though it was the first time for them both, Judy and David had decided against a church wedding because at the time they were both agnostics. The reception was a well-attended affair, for a hundred or so people, at Mancheter's five-star Midland Hotel. David and Judy had invited a few close friends and family but the rest of the guests were from work.

The wedding was the first time David and Judy had seen some of their friends for months. They'd both left their jobs at Granada in the last months of 1973 to go in search of excitement Stateside.

'We'd gone to America to find fame, fortune and a bit of adventure,' says David. 'We did a lot of travelling but ended up living in some cockroach-infested flat in New York.'

The idea had been for the couple to find work as journalists. 'But after five months we ended up not being able to get any work at all,' says David. 'So we came back to England and signed on the dole.'

But not for long. Soon afterwards David landed a job as a reporter at Anglia Television in Norwich. Judy was thrilled to be going with him. They'd had a tough few months since getting back from America and David's new job was a fantastic start to married life for them. The couple bought a house just behind St Martin's in the Fields church in the centre of Norwich. It was less than 500 yards away from the Anglia building which meant that David could walk to the office and Judy could walk to the town hall where she had managed to find work as a secretary.

But she was never going to be happy as a secretary. She'd only been in Norwich six months when she talked her way into a job with Anglia as an on-screen presenter. It was a big break for the girl with no journalistic training who had only ever worked as a researcher when she was at Granada. Judy was proud of herself, and rightly so. Not only was it her first reporting job, but she was one of the few women at the time that Anglia had ever taken on as an on-screen reporter.

To everyone working in the Anglia newsroom, David and Judy seemed like the ideal couple. He was the rock of the relationship, while Judy was the fun, light-hearted side of it. Each enjoyed the fact that the other was clever and they complemented each other perfectly. What's more, they were young and in love.

Guy Adams, who still works at Anglia, was a friend of the Henshaws. 'At the time they seemed to be a good match,' he says. 'Although, after a while, I could see that Judy was beginning to feel that David was a little dull for her. We used to have dinner at each other's houses. Both she and David were quite serious-minded at that time. They both had socialist leanings although they weren't overtly political. I remember Judy being a very good reporter.'

It was while they were both still working at Anglia that the couple's twin boys, Tom and Dan, were born on 2 March

1977. They were very much loved, much wanted children. But, as any new mother knows, it is difficult enough to cope with the demands of *one* newborn baby, let alone two. The young Judy had double the work, double the stress. She never went back to work at Anglia.

'I know she found it extremely hard,' says Guy Adams.

And it got harder. Because soon after the boys were born, David was offered a job with the BBC back in Manchester on the *File on Four* programme.

So, after three years, the couple moved out of their little house behind the church and back to Manchester where they bought a large, post-war, four-bedroomed house in Fallowfields. It was just yards away from the house in Birchfields Road where Judy had lived with her parents. It was a big, comfortable, friendly home but David's new job took him away from it a lot in those first few months after they left Norwich. That left a tense and anxious Judy at home, literally holding her two very beautiful, but none the less exhausting, babies.

For a while she was happy to stay at home and be a full-time mum. She wanted to be with her sons as they went through all those important early stages. It was a time she knew would never come again and she wanted to make the most of it. But after three years of being a housewife and mum, Judy realised she was hankering after a chance to go back to work. She had never been especially ambitious but she did enjoy the cut and thrust of television. She liked the constant banter and the fun. Judy wanted some action. It had been a good idea to take time out with the boys. She had watched them grow from babies into small boys with great big personalities. But now she was stagnating.

Judy had to do an eight-minute audition to get back on to Granada as an on-screen reporter. The brief was to talk straight to camera about any subject under the sun. Lots of people talked about themselves: their ambitions, their lives so far. Judy wanted to be different. She wanted to talk about something that would make her stand out from the rest. So, without faltering, this gorgeous, sexy blonde launched into an eight-minute speech about Manchester United. Judy had grown up listening to her two brothers rave about the team they loved. Old Trafford had been a second home to her. She knew enough about the Red Devils to talk about them for eight hours, let alone eight minutes.

Her screen test was stunning. The men at *Granada Reports* couldn't believe that this beautiful blonde knew more about the local football team than they did. But it had done the trick. She'd made her mark and done more than enough to convince the editor, Rod Caird, that she was the person for the job.

Bob Greaves and Bob Smithies were the frontmen for *Granada Reports* when Judy came back in 1980. The only other on-screen woman at the time was a Liverpool University graduate called Lis Howell.

'I remember Judy bouncing back into that newsroom after three years out,' says Lindsay Charlton. 'And she was gorgeous. She had a shock of blonde hair, a Rubenesque figure she was dazzling. I suppose it's a bit clichéd but after three years at home looking after two small boys, Judy was back in that media world again, and she looked like she was loving it.'

Says Lis Howell: 'I remember Judy coming back into the office having been away for three years and there was a Jewish girl there at the time who, as soon as she saw Judy, said something in Hebrew. I can't remember what the word was but it meant that Judy had a charmed life.'

And she had. Because, within weeks of being back at Granada, she caught the eye of programme controller Mike Scott, who said he wanted Judy on screen as a presenter. Some people were surprised at this speedy promotion, though not everybody.

'Judy had a very definite on-screen presence,' says Lindsay Charlton, now a presenter at London Weekend Television. 'I don't think there was any real resentment at her move to the screen. It was just a part of Granada's melting-pot policy, in which different people with different talents would be put together to come up with something special on screen.'

Judy's meteoric rise to presenter was noticed by some people to coincide with a change in direction by colleague Lis Howell.

'Lis was a bright woman. She rethought her career and changed direction to become one of the most powerful executives in television,' says one TV insider.

The early-eighties was an exciting time for the staff on *Granada Reports*. It was made by people with an exhilarating range of talents, which is why the programme was often thought to be breaking new ground with its wit and irreverence.

Says Lindsay Charlton: 'I remember that in the week before Charles and Di got married *Granada Reports* had a "Stuff the Royal Wedding" week. We asked people who were sick to death of hearing about it to come up with ideas of where they could be on the big day so they wouldn't hear sight or sound of the nuptials.

'There was another famous morning when a producer saw an article in *The Times* which said that sheep are more intelligent than we give them credit for. *Granada Reports* rang up a farmer and asked him if they could borrow fifty sheep. The sheep were then brought to the back of the Granada building and a pen put up on the studio floor. Then the programme opened with presenter Tony Wilson saying, "Hey, there's a report in *The Times* saying that sheep are intelligent. Right, let's see whether they can do *The Times* crossword." And with that he threw the paper in the pen and moved straight on to the next item.

'Yes, there were lots of complaints. Some viewers would support what we were doing at the time, some would think it was outrageous. But *Granada Reports* was unlike any other regional programme. They wanted people with wild creative ideas and people were not punished if some of those ideas turned out to be mistakes.'

Judy was enjoying life back at Granada, and she was turning out to be a good presenter. 'She was jolly clever – in fact, she did a brilliant medical series for me, quite brilliant,' says a producer who was working on *Granada Reports* at the time. 'But she was very clear about her status – she was a presenter and no one was going to make her do anything other than that.

'She did some fantastic things on screen but Judy was never

one to be tramping outside in the cold and the rain. She wasn't vain but she did spend a lot of time walking round the office with a hairdryer in her hand. She was very conscious of needing to look good, and she'd often phone up and say she couldn't come in till the afternoon because she was ill or overtired.'

With a home, a husband and two demanding small children to cope with, as well as a tough on-screen role, it is perhaps unsurprising that Judy was occasionally tired and worried about looking her best while, no doubt, the usual domestic traumas were taking place behind the scenes.

'Having said that, you could never fault her on her intelligence or her ability to grasp things,' remembers the same producer. 'She always did her homework on whatever subject we were going to be talking about.'

Judy was sometimes nicknamed CBB. The acronym stood for 'Can't Be Bothered', a phrase which apparently originated from the early days when she was sharing a flat with one of Granada's make-up girls.

'Judy had a reputation for being pretty lazy,' says one of the other presenters at *Granada Reports*. 'She couldn't really be bothered with very much. I, on the other hand, could. And the idea that she has now presented one of the most difficult, gruelling, high-pressure shows on television – which frankly I don't think I'd be able to take for more than a month – I find very amusing.'

In spite of her CBB reputation, Judy was impressive on screen and in 1981 landed the job of presenting Granada's network programme, *Reports Action*.

Joan Bakewell and Anna Ford had been in the hot seat before her so the young Manchester mum had a lot to live up to. The show's brief was to 'turn viewers into doers', and Judy's job, together with co-presenter Bob Greaves, was to mobilise the millions watching to help the needy. At the time Judy was unconcerned by comparisons with her predecessors. 'I'd rather be doing this than *News at Ten*,' she said. 'This kind of live television is much more fun.'

But even though Judy's career was going great guns and no one could fault her at her job, her unusual dress sense was legendary at the office. Judy loved wearing big swinging dirndl skirts, wide, waist-clinching belts, and skimpy, tight-fitting tops.

A production assistant at the time says, 'When Judy was working on a show called *Scramble*, it was always a joke that the producer, a lovely man called Jim Walker, would tell people in the office to tell Judy, gently of course, that she had to stop wearing those wide unfashionable skirts when she was on screen.'

Although Jim Walker may not have thought much of Judy's dress sense, he says that where work was concerned, she was a trouper: 'I remember once she was doing an important piece on camera. I could see that her eyes had started to water badly but I didn't know what was happening. Anyway, she finished the link and we went straight into the film. It was only afterwards Judy told me that her contact lens had moved around and was sticking directly into her eye. Without anyone realising what was happening, she had carried on without letting the tears stream down her face. She was very good, and still is in my opinion. She's cool in a crisis.'

But fame, albeit regional fame, meant some people reacted differently to Judy. Women in the office who had once considered themselves her friends began to think they were no longer of interest to the presenter whose fame was beginning to spread in the north-west.

One ex-friend claims, 'Judy used to be one of the girls until she became a presenter. After that you'd pass her in the corridor and she'd be hard pushed to say hello.' Of course, Judy might have been just trying to remember her lines.

Another friend, Irene McGlashin, who worked in the production office, remembers 'going to her house one night. She and David were still married and they were having a party. She had only just started back at *Granada Reports* a few weeks earlier, having had a few years off, and she desperately wanted to make a good impression. She was particularly nervous at the time because the unions were very militant at Granada. In those days, if a reporter did not abide by the union rules, their material just wasn't transmitted. Judy was frightened by that. I spent half the night explaining the union rules to her, about what you could and couldn't do, and reassuring her that everything would be OK.

'I realised then that Judy was very clever. She always needed lots of reassurance, which she always got from both men and women.'

Maybe Judy found that as she rose within the Granada organisation she had less and less in common with those friends whose company and advice she had relied upon when she first started in television. On the other side of the coin, old friends often find the widening career gulf hard to handle. This is when innocent behaviour may well be misinterpreted.

Former Granada colleague Lindsay Charlton, who has himself achieved celebrity as a presenter, knows what it is like to stand up to the merciless scrutiny of camera and public alike, and how this can affect a television personality. 'The thing you have to understand about Judy is that she's a great performer but she suffers from anxiety. She goes through huge post-mortems after programmes, crosses every t and dots every i. She worries about every line.'

This pursuit of professional excellence eventually began to tell on Judy's private life. Cracks were beginning to appear in her marriage.

But for a while life carried on as normal. Until one day in 1982, when Richard Madeley walked into Granada and changed Judy Finnigan's life for ever.

3 Richard

RICHARD MADELEY SPENDS 23 ¼ hours of every day with his wife. They get up at 6am. They travel to work. They do *This Morning*. They come home. The only break in this constant 'togetherness' is a brief 45-minute period when Richard goes to buy food for the evening meal. When living in Manchester he used to cycle to the shops near his home in Didsbury.

'We are like two prisoners in a cell,' he has said of their self-imposed sentence. And they are.

It is an existence that would stifle most couples. The isolation, the lack of stimulus, the absence of friends, and just the sheer unremitting sight of each other day after day would be enough to drive most couples into the divorce courts. But this is not the first time Richard Madeley has lived so close to the woman he loves. He did it once before in another life, with another wife.

'He told me that he needed to be with me *all* the time,' says Lynda Madeley, the wife Richard left for Judy Finnigan. 'He had to make sure that I was with him constantly.'

Richard Madeley was born on 13 May 1957 in Romford, Essex. Emergency petrol rationing had recently ended in Britain and, just a few miles away in the City of London, the Suez Canal Company had resurrected the idea of building a channel tunnel that would run between England and France. But the Madeleys didn't have time to consider the ridiculous and unlikely notion that a tunnel would ever run under the sea. All they could think about was their newborn son.

Richard Madeley's middle class childhood was spent in leafy

Brentwood with his sister, Liz, and parents Chris and Claire, first in a three-bedroomed house in St John's Avenue, Marley, and later, as his father prospered as a PR for Ford Motors, in a much roomier Victorian house in Hartswood Road, Brentford.

It's hard to tell when ambition first took hold of the lanky lad with the mop of glossy brown hair. Friends and acquaintances remark that, from being a teenager, Richard has been driven by an unquenchable thirst for success. Those who have worked with him have watched from the sidelines as he scaled the career ladder. It has been a dizzyingly speedy ascent.

As a teenager he enrolled for a year-long course in journalism at Harlow College in Bishop's Stortford but left less than halfway through because, as far as he was concerned, the only way to learn to *be* a journalist was to *do* the job and not just read books about it.

Chris Madeley was the inspiration behind his handsome son's choice of career. He was a strong, loving father and Richard worshipped the tall, elegant man with his shock of black hair and kind if mischievous eyes that twinkled behind dark-rimmed spectacles.

Richard saw the comfortable lifestyle Chris Madeley had provided for his family, first with a career in newspapers and later as PR at Ford Motors. He looked up to this caring, emotional man who found it so easy to express his feelings and whose deep voice belied his soft heart.

Richard's first job after leaving college in 1974 was as a rookie reporter on the *Brentwood Argus*, whose offices were just a few miles from his home. Even at the age of seventeen, Richard knew that if he worked hard and got his by-line in the paper, he wouldn't have to spend long in the dusty, parochial environment of the *Argus*. Some of the reporters had been stagnating there for twenty years. But that wasn't going to happen to him. He was destined for bigger things.

In those first few months on the *Argus*, Richard worked as if his life depended on it. He was first into the office every day and last to leave at night. It was a pattern, a strongly developed work ethic, that would stay with him for many years. He reported on golden weddings. He covered local fêtes. He even sat in on the odd council meeting. But all the while the young hack was on the lookout for the 'Big Story'. Richard had only been on the *Argus* a matter of weeks before he got it.

Until then, the young reporter with his tousled hair and ankle-length trench coat with its 'journo's' upturned collar, had caused some amusement among the older scribes on the patch. They'd decided that if he spent as much time trying to *be* a reporter as he did trying to *look* like one, he'd soon be Journalist of the Year. He had the coat. He had the cigarettes. All he needed was 'PRESS' stamped across his forehead and then no one would be in any doubt as to what he did for a living. But as they laughed and joked, Richard Madeley just kept right on working, touring round his patch on a noisy little moped.

He didn't care what anyone else thought. He was going places, and the guys who thought he was funny now would be laughing on the other side of their faces in a few years' time.

'Richard definitely believed in himself,' says Peter Baker, who was a reporter on the *Brentwood Gazette* at the time. 'And he was an extremely conscientious and determined reporter.'

Peter remembers the night Richard found his big story: 'There had been an horrific accident on the A127 road on the old Halfway House roundabout next to the M25 flyover. It was a terrible night. A big storm had broken and the rain was coming down so hard you could barely see two feet in front of your face.

'A lot of local reporters were already at the scene of the accident. Suddenly, through the storm, we heard the familiar pop-popping sound. I knew it was Richard. I recognised the sound of his moped.'

The young Madeley was drenched from head to foot when he finally clambered off his moped just yards from the scene of the accident. His green mac clung to him like a sodden blanket. His usually immaculate hair streamed from his head in saturated rats' tails. And when he pulled out his notebook to start writing his story, it was so wet it just disintegrated in his hands.

'But he was determined to have that story,' says Peter. 'He'd travelled miles in the driving rain to get to the accident and he had no intention of missing out just because he had nothing to write on. He was wet through but he didn't seem to notice. He just squelched his way over to me and asked if he could borrow a few sheets of paper to write his story.'

Richard's reputation spread among the other local reporters as, week after week, he kept coming up with bright new exclusives. It was in 1976 that he got the break he'd been waiting for: he was offered a job as a reporter on BBC Radio Cumbria based in Carlisle. It was a huge achievement for an eighteen year old, but Richard had worked hard and this was his reward. His other reward to himself, and one which cost him every last penny of his savings, was a gleaming white Spitfire sports car which had the unfortunate number plate RPP, which friends mischieviously suggested stood for 'Richard – Perfect Person'.

With as many clothes as he could cram into the restricted boot of the Spitfire, a few of his favourite Eagles albums and his beloved guitar, Richard set off for Carlisle. It was a long journey, more than 300 miles, so there was plenty of time to plan his bright new future with the BBC. Richard had already found himself a bedsit in Warwick Road which was in the centre of Carlisle. It was a huge rambling Victorian house which contained a ground-floor flat, two bedsits and a tiny attic room.

The young reporter could barely contain his excitement. As he combed the streets of Carlisle in his new sports car, searching for Warwick Road, he contemplated what lay ahead. He had his independence in his own bedsit. He had an exciting new career in broadcasting. And just the day before he had celebrated his nineteenth birthday.

Lynda Hooley lived in the ground-floor flat in Warwick Road. It was hard to believe that this strikingly pretty girl, with the heart-shaped face and eyes the colour of coffee beans, was 26 years old. A petite 5ft 3ins, and weighing just eight stone, she could easily have passed for eighteen.

Lynda had lived in Carlisle since the age of thirteen, having been born in Montreal, Canada. Her father had been stationed in England during the war where he had met and married his wife. When peace was declared the two of them moved back to Montreal to live and start a family. But not long after Lynda was born, her mother, plagued by homesickness, begged her husband to take them back to England.

Lynda was less than a year old when the family returned. They couldn't afford to buy a house straight away so they rented one belonging to Lynda's grandfather in Darlington. The family stayed there until their pretty, dark-haired daughter was seven. After five years in Lincoln where her father worked for Shellmex, the Hooleys eventually settled in Carlisle.

The young Lynda was not particularly ambitious, which was just as well as her life was plagued by ill health which meant long, painful spells in hospital. As a child, she suffered complications with sinus problems and asthma which left her with a chronic hearing problem. She was almost totally deaf in one ear and had reduced hearing in the other, which not even two major operations had been able to improve. Then, in her early twenties, she was rushed into hospital to have a kidney removed.

Despite her ill health, Lynda still managed to enjoy life. She had latched on to the tail end of the Merry England movement and belonged to an altogether gentler and more refined group of hippies than today's New Agers. With her long floaty skirts, her headbands and scoop-necked cheesecloth tops, Lynda was the antithesis of the smart young man who knocked on the door of the Warwick Road house on that chilly May evening and announced he was the new tenant. Lynda had been told by the landlord that he had rented the vacant bedsits to two young professionals, one a chap from the local Metal Box Company's personnel department, the other a young reporter from London who was starting work on Radio Cumbria.

When she first clapped eyes on the immaculately dressed man who stood in the hallway with the collar of his trench coat turned up and his belt pulled fashionably tight around his waist, Lynda decided this man couldn't possibly be the journalist. He had to be the young executive from the Metal Box Company.

A couple of days later she was sweeping the hallway outside her flat. It was Saturday so she was dressed in tattered old jeans and a cheesecloth smock, and her glossy, dark hair had been plaited Indian squaw-style.

In a voice brimming with confidence, the young man whom she'd seen a few days earlier came out on to the stairs and told her he was Richard Madeley from Radio Cumbria, that he had moved in upstairs, and would she like to go out for a drink sometime?

Lynda was taken unawares. He wasn't really her type. She liked rugged, craggy men with irregular features and a five o'clock shadow. She muttered something that enabled her to dash back to the flat without his being able to see how scruffy she looked. She might not fancy him, but she didn't want him to think she was a mess.

The following Sunday Lynda and Richard found themselves alone in the house. All the other tenants had gone away for the weekend and he suggested that as they were the only ones not doing anything, they might go out for a drink together. This time Lynda said yes.

'I decided he didn't look quite so frightening with his jeans on,' she remembers. 'Although he still looked pretty formal because he was wearing a crisp white shirt with them. It was the kind of shirt you wore with a suit, not the kind a nineteen year old would wear tucked into his 501s.'

Lynda decided to take Richard to a pub in Carlisle called the Coach House. 'I'd seen him carrying his guitar when he moved in,' she says, 'so I thought he'd like the Coach House. It was a really trendy pub that had jazz and folk music on alternate nights.'

Richard and Lynda laughed and drank and talked all afternoon. The afternoon turned into evening and they discovered they had much in common. The relationship developed. When Richard had finished working at Radio Carlisle and Lynda had shut up shop at clothes store Chelsea Girl, where she was deputy manageress, the two of them would head for the Coach House where Richard liked nothing better than jamming with the locals.

'He had a lovely soft voice, a bit like Al Stewart,' says Lynda. 'He would always take his guitar and sing along to whoever was listening.'

If the young Richard was beginning to make an impression on Lynda Hooley, he was making an even bigger impression at the offices of Radio Cumbria. None of the other reporters could quite believe this lanky, baby-faced lad who had more confidence than the rest of them put together. Richard told them all that his ambition lay in national television and that he intended to be a current affairs presenter in the mould of Robin Day. He had studied the technique of the big-name presenters, their voices, their style of dress, convinced that he could do it better. He would even memorise scripts and speak into the radio microphone, practising for the day he went into television.

It was, perhaps, this dream of being a TV star that made him take even more care of his already immaculate appearance. He would spray his hair with Lynda's lacquer and very occasionally tone down the colour of his lips with pale pink lipstick because he thought it made him look more tanned.

Former Radio Cumbria colleague Nigel Holmes said in an interview with the *Daily Mirror* that Richard 'wanted to be famous. He wanted recognition and was very open about it'.

Tony Baker, who is now political correspondent for the BBC in Newcastle, then reading the news at Radio Cumbria, says, 'He was a really young lad when he arrived in Carlisle but he was clearly going places. He was immensely confident and never had a single moment's doubt that he would make it. But I liked him a lot. He was an engaging sort of bloke.'

Engaging he might have been, precocious he almost certainly was, but Richard Madeley was also good. So good that at nineteen, as well as being a reporter, he was also offered a producing job. It made him the youngest producer the station had ever had. 'He fought to get the best programmes,' remembers Nigel Holmes. 'He went hell for leather to get the Sunday morning request show because he knew it had the highest ratings. And, despite the fact he was the youngest bloke on the station, he got it.'

By then Richard and Lynda were living together in a bungalow they had rented in Red Dial, near Wigton. But this was the seventies, and although lots of young people had opted to live together, marriage was still seen as the only true indicator of maturity and respectability. Richard asked Lynda what she thought about getting married. They'd been talking about a future together now for months. He had left Lynda in no doubt that she was the one he wanted to marry.

'He wanted us to get married in April,' says Lynda, 'but I was determined to leave it until later in the year. I wanted our wedding to be special.'

As far as Richard was concerned, he and Lynda had decided to get married and it might as well be sooner rather than later. They were in love. Why wait?

It was this hasty attitude that had already concerned her at the start of their relationship. It had begun gently enough. But, almost without her noticing, Richard had started to move his clothes and his toiletries from his messy bedsit into her spotless little flat.

'I just woke up one day after we'd been going out for a few weeks, and I panicked,' Lynda remembers. 'I saw his socks, his underpants and his shirts all strewn over my flat and I realised he was creeping in on me. Everything was happening too fast. Richard was racing the relationship. But I'd just come out of a long-term thing with someone and I needed time and space. I wasn't head over heels in love with him at that stage, although I knew we had something special. I didn't want to spoil that, so while he was out at work that day I moved all of his things back into the bedsit.

'Usually I would never go into his room upstairs. It was a typical teenager's room. The curtains were never open, his bed was always unmade, he never did any washing or ironing, and there were always empty jars of Sutherland salmon paste lying all over the place.'

When Richard came home that night he was stunned. But Lynda soon realised she couldn't hold him at arm's length for long. 'I gave in in the end,' she says. 'There came a point when I just looked at him and I was besotted. It had taken a few months to get to know the man beneath the arrogant, assured exterior, but once I had, I fell head over heels in love. I would look at him and just melt because he was so lovely to me.'

One day Richard came home and said there was a bungalow that had been vacated by someone who had just left the radio station. He asked Lynda to move in with him.

'He was very impulsive,' she says. 'And, by that stage, so was I. We knew we were jumping on this great big tidal wave that could throw us off at any moment but we just decided to go with it. In my heart, I knew then that Richard was going to be *the* man in my life.'

It was an idyllic time for the young lovers. The summer of 1976 was one of the hottest on record and Richard and Lynda took full advantage of it. They sunbathed naked in the sand dunes at Silloth. They made easy, lazy love on those scorching afternoons, and afterwards, as they lay together on the sand, they planned their future which, way back then, looked as rosy as the setting sun.

'Richard was incredibly romantic,' says Lynda. 'He would sing to me when we were at home together. He would read me stories at bedtime. He loved Laurie Lee and would read me *Cider With Rosie* and *As I Walked Out One Midsummer Morning*. I remember we danced in the streets that summer when the rains came. We'd had months without any. And when finally they came Richard and I raced out into the street in our bare feet and danced and danced in the middle of Carlisle until we were ready to drop. We were two crazy kids who were madly in love. When Richard falls in love there are no half measures. It is 150 per cent. It was like that for me too.'

The couple got engaged at Christmas when they went home to see Richard's parents. Lynda's engagement ring was a tiny gold band with three garnets. It cost just £13. Richard's was a signet ring.

'We went to stay with Richard's parents in Brentwood,' says

Lynda. 'We put our rings, which were all wrapped up, on the tree. And on Christmas morning, when the whole family sat down to a formal breakfast, we took them down and told everyone we were getting married. His parents were shocked because everything had happened so quickly. But all we could think about was how happy we were.'

The happy couple were married at St Hilda's Church, Westward, Wigton, on 31 July 1977. It was a beautiful day. The sun shone down on the picturesque little church on the edge of the vast Cumbrian moors overlooking the Lake District. But Lynda wasn't interested in the scenery or the weather. She was marrying the man she loved. The sunshine was a bonus.

She'd bought her cream Laura Ashley wedding dress, with its delicate crochet edging around collar and cuffs, for £15 in a sale in London.

'I fell in love with it as soon as I saw it,' she says. 'But I had to show it to Richard first. He had to approve it otherwise I wouldn't have been able to wear it. But he loved it, especially when he discovered I'd got a bargain because he was paying!'

As they were so hard up, they had decided to keep the guest list small. Only four people were invited: Chris and Claire Madeley, and Lynda's mother and stepfather. Before the wedding, Richard's dad had sat him down and asked his son if he was sure he was doing the right thing. He had only just turned twenty and he had his whole life ahead of him. More importantly, he had only ever had one girlfriend before Lynda. Work had always been a bigger turn-on than women for Richard. Until he met Lynda.

But even though he was madly in love with her, Richard had already warned Lynda about the very real possibility of his infidelity. 'He told me that in his line of work, especially in television, marriages were destined for divorce because there was a lot of temptation. Looking back, I think he was warning me of what was to come. But I had already decided that this was not going to affect our relationship. I thought that what we had was so strong it could never be touched by another woman. This was at a time when we were ecstatically happy.

We were the people who danced naked in the snow together in winter and made love on the beach in the summer. Why was he talking about the temptations of other women?'

Despite the father and son tête-à-tête, the wedding went off without a hitch. Richard's mum and dad looked on proudly as their son, so handsome in his smart black suit, his white shirt and black kipper tie with multi-coloured stripes, made his vows to the woman he loved. Lynda looked adoringly back at him. She had no doubts, no reservations. This was right, and now she understood what people meant when they talked about marriages made in heaven. She knew she looked beautiful, not just because Richard told her so but because she *felt* beautiful. She'd had her long dark hair crimped, and instead of a veil had chosen to wear just a simple halo of white daisies. The dress looked stunning, as she'd known it would, and in her hand she carried a little silk bouquet of daisies, forget-me-nots and lemon sweetpeas.

'I was on cloud nine all day,' she remembers. 'It was, quite simply, the most wonderful day of my life. I knew even when I woke up that morning it was going to be a magical day. Butterflies play a very significant part in my life and when any momentous event takes place, whether it be happy or sad, a butterfly always comes to me. It happened on my wedding day. I was sitting by my window, doing my hair and putting on my make-up, when a beautiful Red Admiral flew in the window and fluttered around my face. I knew then that everything was going to be perfect.'

There was no official photographer because Richard and Lynda couldn't afford one. Both sets of parents did their best with cameras brought from home, although it meant there was always one of them missing from the photo. The reception was held at the nearby Trout Beck Hotel in Cockermouth. The bill came to just £30 for the six of them and afterwards everyone went back to the little bungalow at Westward where the wedding cake, made by Richard's mum and decorated with little forget-me-not flowers, was waiting.

Because money was so tight and they were saving up to buy their own house, the happy couple had decided that instead of a proper honeymoon they would use Chris and Claire Madeley's home in Essex as a base so they could go to London every day for sightseeing trips. A second week was to be spent in Wells, Somerset, where a friend of the family had offered them a static caravan for a week.

But the honeymoon was doomed. Something terrible was about to happen – something that would change their lives for ever.

Chris Madeley had just waved off his son and his new bride on the second week of their honeymoon. He was feeling happy. It had been good having them to stay for the week, and seeing them so happy together. But he was feeling very tired. There had been the excitement of the wedding, and before that he'd been haring round the country, giving talks and lectures for Ford on a crippling schedule – Scotland one day, the Midlands the next. No wonder he felt like taking a rest.

The first day of the honeymoon in Somerset started with a row. 'I can't even remember what it was about,' says Lynda. 'But because the argument had left us both feeling angry we'd decided to go our separate ways for a few minutes to cool off. I remember it was exactly 1pm when we turned our backs on each other and walked in different directions.'

At precisely 1.05 the honeymooners fell into each other's arms again, hugging and laughing and promising never to fight again.

At 1.07pm, Chris Madeley died in his wife's arms of a massive heart attack. He was just 49 years old.

The young couple had had a glorious day, their quarrel long since forgotten. The sun blazed relentlessly down on their gently tanning bodies as they swam and sunbathed and promised they would love one another for ever.

But as they walked back to the caravan site late that afternoon, arms wrapped round one another, the owner of the site was waiting for them in reception. She looked solemn as she told them they had to ring Richard's home urgently. As they stood crushed in a phone box and dialled the number in

Essex, they shivered despite the evening sun blazing through the glass. Something terrible must have happened.

The journey back to Essex was horrendous. Lynda cried in great racking sobs all the way. Richard sat stony-faced at the wheel. He didn't cry; he couldn't, the shock ran so deep. He had worshipped his father and now could not take in the fact that he had gone.

'I don't think we even talked,' says Lynda. 'We were both in a complete daze. Chris Madeley was a very special man. He was like a father to me and I felt closer to him than I did to my own. He found it easy to show emotion, to show that he cared. I loved him for that.

'Richard was utterly devastated by his father's death. They were best friends. He used to ring his dad every day to tell him what story he had been doing and ask him for ideas. Chris was very proud of his son and Richard was very proud of his father. They were able to talk about anything and everything and there was barely a minute of the day when each didn't know what the other was doing.'

When they reached the house, Richard's mother was waiting with his sister, Liz. Lynda, who was suffering from a stress-induced migraine attack, left them alone together and went to bed.

Chris Madeley was buried on what should have been the second week of his son's honeymoon. There had been no warnings of any heart trouble, no previous scares, but he had been a heavy smoker who, until he had given up at the age of 38, had smoked 60 a day.

'Chris's death shattered Richard's life,' says Lynda. 'It also shattered the first year of our marriage.' They returned to Cumbria. 'But our relationship was different,' she says. 'We still had good times but there were also bad times. I knew Richard was desperately missing his father.'

It was just ten months into his marriage, and Richard was still working at Radio Cumbria, when things started to go seriously wrong between the newlyweds. Maybe it was insecurity caused by the devastating blow of his father's death that made the still deeply distressed Richard turn to another woman for comfort. Chris Madeley had been a stabilising and loving influence on his only son's life. He had been his rock, the person Richard could always turn to for advice. Without him the younger man was lost – not just professionally but emotionally as well. And maybe, in his confusion, Richard decided life was too short not to take what you want, when you want.

'I realised something was wrong when he started taking a change of clothes to work,' says Lynda. 'He told me he had to go out to meetings after work. I didn't believe him, of course. He had never had to go to meetings before.'

By this time they had moved out of the bungalow and into Carlton Hill House where Lynda had landed the job of house-keeper to a wealthy old lady who needed domestic help. Free accommodation in the form of a flat attached to the big house came with the job, which suited Richard and Lynda as they were saving hard for a home of their own.

Lynda was happy here. A born homemaker, she relished the work of cleaning the old lady's collection of antique grand-father clocks, polishing the mahogany dining table and great oak dresser, and sweeping the old flagstone floors.

But while Lynda worked to save the money they needed to buy their first home, Richard became increasingly distant and preoccupied. When she confronted him with the fact that she believed he was having an affair, he denied it. He said he wasn't having an affair but that he wanted to move out for a while because he needed some space.

'I'd always told Richard that if he fell in love with someone else I wanted *him* to tell me, I never wanted to hear it from someone else. I'm not a possessive woman and I've never believed in hanging on to a relationship when one partner wants out. It's pointless. So when Richard asked for time and space, I gave it to him.'

A few weeks later Lynda was out shopping when she spotted Richard. He was carrying a box of glasses and a tablecloth which, she assumed, he had bought in readiness for a romantic supper with the other woman.

'I don't have an ounce of jealousy in my body,' says Lynda. 'But when I saw him that day I was utterly heartbroken.'

A close friend of Richard and Lynda's, Maureen Clark, says that although Richard might have been having an affair, he wasn't predatory when it came to women. 'What I saw was that he and Lynda were very happy. Obviously there were girls who fancied him but he never touched them. There was one girl who even told one of the lads in our crowd that she wanted him, and when Richard found out he literally ran away. He was so stressed about it that he lit a fag from the coal fire and practically singed his eyebrows off. I liked him. He was a super person to have around.'

But, for whatever reason, he was no longer with Lynda and she tried to get on with her life as best she could. She went to Edinburgh where she did some hair modelling which resulted in a whole new look for her. Because of the break up, she also lost a lot of weight.

'The next time Richard saw me he did a double take,' she says.

Before the split, Richard and Lynda had booked a holiday in Italy which was supposed to have made up for the honeymoon that had ended so disastrously. Although the two of them were still living apart, they decided they would go on holiday and see if they could save their marriage. The coach taking them to London was leaving Carlisle station at midnight. They agreed to meet there.

Lynda decided she would pack and then get a few hours' sleep before she met Richard at the station. But in the event she was so excited at the prospect of seeing him again that she couldn't close her eyes.

She rang a couple of friends and asked them to come over and bring a bottle of wine. 'After we'd finished the wine we decided to go to a club which was right next door to the bus station. I could get on the bus straight from there.'

The first thing Lynda saw when she walked into that dark, smoky club was her husband wrapped around another woman. Lynda exploded. All the hurt, the pain, the anger came flooding back. She stomped over to where they sat, nose to nose, and slapped the woman across the face.

'I called her a cow,' Lynda remembers. Then she turned to her husband, who had never seen this side of her temper, and shouted, 'As for you, Richard Madeley, don't bother coming to the station. I am going on this holiday on my own, and when I come back we are getting a divorce!' And with that she turned on her heel and marched out.

Within minutes he was at her side, begging forgiveness. And when Lynda looked into his pleading face she knew that, despite what he had put her through over the past weeks, she still loved him. She would forgive him. She had no other choice.

'After all those weeks apart he was back with me. We kissed all the way to London. I found myself falling in love with him all over again.'

Italy was everything Lynda had dreamed it would be. It was the honeymoon they'd never had.

'We were ecstatically happy. We did silly, romantic, wonderful things on that holiday. We sunbathed. We took moonlit walks by the sea. We hired a scooter and drove into a dozen sunsets together. I loved him so much that I didn't want to waste precious time talking about why he had gone off. We were back together again and I wanted my marriage to work more than anything in the world. I had to trust him if we were going to stay together.'

Just a few weeks after their return from Italy, Richard and Lynda were invited to dinner by another couple. The husband worked with Richard at Radio Cumbria. The meal was great fun. Soon after it, the host announced he had to leave to go and do the nightshift in the newsroom. Instead of breaking up the party, Richard and Lynda decided to sleep over so they could have a few more drinks. At 12.30 Lynda decided she'd had enough. She was tired and had to get up early in the morning. She left Richard and their hostess drinking and chatting. At about 3.30 in the morning she woke up, needing the loo.

'They lived in a funny little cottage. The bathroom was downstairs.' Sleepily she made her way down. She was rubbing her eyes when she stumbled into the kitchen and saw something that turned her stomach: her husband and their hostess, her friend, in the throes of a passionate embrace.

'They were making an absolute meal of each other. I couldn't believe what I was seeing. They were kissing and their hands were all over each other.'

Lynda stood in the doorway, unable to believe what was in front of her eyes. She was frightened to move in case she fainted. It was just a few weeks since the episode at the station followed by that wonderful romantic holiday. How could he do this to her again?

It was the woman who saw Lynda first. She tapped Richard on the shoulder.

'He looked at me and I saw the colour drain from his face,' says Lynda. 'He let out a big groan and just said, "Oh, God!" The two of them couldn't apologise enough. Over and over again they just kept repeating, "Sorry, sorry, sorry." ' Richard told her: 'Forgive us, we were no better than dogs in the street.'

Lynda went back upstairs to bed. He followed her. He tried to cuddle her, but she didn't want him near her.

'It was then he said he needed me to be with him all the time because he couldn't trust himself,' says Lynda. 'He said, from then on, wherever he went, I had to be there to protect him from temptation.'

Shortly after this Richard landed a job as a reporter on Border Television. One of his new colleagues there was Lis Howell. In 1977, like Richard, she was a Border reporter.

'We had some really good laughs,' she says. 'The thing about Richard is that he is a genuinely charming man and that takes your mind off the fact that he is quite brainy and can be very, very funny. He was one of the best colleagues I ever worked with. He was not only good at what he did, he was no trouble, nor was he political.

'I remember we did a Thatcher election together and worked all through the night. It was good to work with him because he is the most organically unsexist man I ever met. He is not a woman's man but he was very good at seeing the woman's point of view, and there aren't many men in television like that. There would have been a lot of men out to "get" a woman like me at that time, but Richard certainly wasn't one of them. It wasn't that he was protective of me, because I would have found that mildly offensive. It was working with an equal.

'He was a tremendously capable man too, and that's one of the things I liked about him. He could go out and make a three-minute film about a chair and it would be good. You get an awful lot of people who go into regional TV who are confused about how to do it. There is a particular skill to it – you have to interview people, then do cut-aways. There are lots of complicated techniques. You are directing, organising and editing a film. And Richard was one of the best.

'He never gave me the impression of wanting to shaft anyone, but we were all very single-minded and ambitious at Border. It wasn't a cosy environment. The pressure was to get on and get out.'

By the time he reached Border, Richard had set his heart on being a presenter and worked constantly on his technique. He studied the men who were at the top of the tree and vowed that one day he would be up there alongside them.

Lynda remembers the first day Richard was recognised in the street, the infallible sign to any broadcaster that he or she is really beginning to make a mark. 'He came rushing into the house, shouting and singing at the top of his voice: "I got recognised! I got recognised!"

'He was like a child he was so excited. He swung me round and round in the kitchen and then he started dancing a little jig all on his own, he was so happy. And I was happy for him too. Yes, Richard was ambitious, exceptionally ambitious maybe. But I think a lot of people were jealous of the fact he was achieving so much while they were just plodding along, doing what they had been doing for years.'

Richard's hard work and attention to detail was also reflected in the care he took over his appearance. Now that he was visible to an audience, everything about him had to be just right.

'He had always spent time in front of the mirror, but when he started working in TV he'd spend hours trying to get his hair exactly right,' Lynda recalls. 'He plastered on so much hair spray that his hair never moved. And he was fastidious about his clothes.

'I remember once we went to see *All the President's Men* starring Robert Redford. In the film Redford was wearing a very pale blue suit, a white shirt, and a red and white spotted silk tie. Richard just fell in love with the whole thing. So we scoured the country till we found a suit and tie exactly like Redford's. It would not have mattered how much the suit cost, Richard was determined to have it. He would not be happy until he had acquired the whole outfit.'

But while Richard was prepared to spend money on his own clothes, the Madeleys' joint finances were still very tight. 'Before we got married he opened a joint bank account and all my wages were paid into it. After the wedding he told me he didn't want me to go to work. He said he didn't want me working anywhere where there were lots of men. I was offered a really good job in a men's boutique but Richard absolutely put his foot down. The thought of me being around men drove him mad.

'I'd always had my own money before I married Richard but even then I was only allowed to spend money on myself within reason. I used to have to sneak things into the house, hide them in the wardrobe and bring them out weeks later pretending I'd had them for months.

'But as soon as I stopped work that was it. Nothing. I never even had a credit card.'

Undoubtedly Richard, as the sole bread-winner, must have felt justified in being angry over what seemed to him extravagant purchases. He believed his clothes and appearance were essential to his job – he had to look smart, and that doesn't come cheap.

In October 1979, Richard landed a job as a reporter with Yorkshire Television. They hadn't long bought their three-bedroomed Victorian house in Eden Place, Carlisle, when it was time to move on again. But this was the job Richard had been waiting for. He was to be a reporter on Yorkshire's nightly news programme, *Calendar*. And one of the first things he did when he got his publicity photos was to give his wife two signed copies. On the back of one of them he wrote: 'Hang on to this. One day it will be worth a lot of money.'

Richard had only been at Yorkshire a couple of months when he rushed home to Lynda with some exciting news. He said that one of his bosses had hinted that Richard Whiteley (now of *Countdown* fame), the undisputed star at the station and the man who had been dubbed 'Mr Yorkshire TV', might be leaving. Richard said he'd been told that if worked hard he could be Whiteley's successor.

'He was thrilled. He'd always wanted to present his own show and Richard Whiteley had his own chat show at Yorkshire. Then Richard decided he'd have to stay ultra squeaky clean. He stopped smoking. He cut down on his drinking. He was always first in the office in the morning and last to leave at night. He wanted to show everyone he was there and meant business.'

But Richard was in for his first big disappointment. On talking to some of his colleagues he discovered that they too had been told of Whiteley's possible departure and been promised that if they worked hard and showed willing, the crown could be theirs. It had been a clever ruse by Richard's bosses to get as much out of their ambitious young reporters as they possibly could. At that stage Richard Whiteley had no intention of leaving, but by hinting he might the show's bosses gambled that all the ambitious young reporters would work flat out, not only to get Whiteley's job but for what it entailed – stardom.

One of the reporters who was in the newsroom when Richard arrived says: 'He didn't have a reputation as a formidable intellect, although he could cover the story of an overturned truck on the A1 with the best of them. He was one of those immaculately good-looking men who had a kind of instinct for intonation and for knowing when to nod in a sympathetic way when he was interviewing. He was an eerie TV natural.

'We all knew him because we all worked in the same office. But we didn't know him at all really. We didn't know what he cared about, what his journalistic beliefs were. He didn't show any interest in politics or corruption. We didn't know how he felt about the big issues.'

But although Richard wasn't rated for any political commitment by his colleagues, it was acknowledged that he never tried to do anyone down. 'He was ambitious,' says one of his Yorkshire colleagues, 'but it was by instinct – not in a predatory way. There was no spite in the man.'

Although Richard had always wanted to be a thrusting current affairs reporter, his Yorkshire colleagues did not believe he was best suited to the role. 'Heavy current affairs was not his forte,' says the reporter who worked with him. 'The news editor would never have dreamed of putting Richard on a story that involved a rocket scientist or quantum physics. We have always found it strange to read that he wanted to be a *World In Action* type of reporter because, when he was here he had no enthusiasm for that kind of work.

'It was interesting to observe Richard at a distance. We all felt that if he was going to become successful it would be as a presenter rather than a reporter. No one at Yorkshire is the least bit surprised by what has happened to him. In fact, it could be said that the bosses here were a bit slow not to spot his kind of talent and sign him up.'

But while his particular style may not have been the envy of everyone at Yorkshire, Richard still turned up every day at the *Calendar* offices determined to make his mark. The first-floor newsroom, with its huge oblong windows which ran the full length of the building, looked down on to Burley Road, Leeds. There were always film cameras rolling there. When directors needed a war-torn alley in Belfast, they came to Burley Road. It was actually used in a few episodes of *Harry's Game* because of its authentic shabbiness.

Every morning reporters would turn up in the newsroom having had to pass through the documentary and science department on their way. The ambitious young reporters always slackened their pace as they passed the 'doco' department, ever hopeful they might be spotted by one of the heads of current affairs and whisked away to cerebral heaven. When they finally reached the newsroom they would be briefed by the waiting researchers on whatever local news story had been assigned for the day.

When the tall, handsome Richard Madeley strolled into the newsroom on his first day there was an initial shiver of excitement among the women on the *Calendar* staff. Hunky men were scarce and there had been rumours that this new Madeley chap was a bit of a looker.

'In a place like *Calendar* there weren't many good-looking men,' says one of the women who was a researcher at the time. 'On the surface he looked to have everything. He had a handsome face, all his own hair, he was charming – but we just couldn't get past the bland exterior to see if there was anything more interesting inside.

'He was a nice bloke and though he wasn't a superbrain he was good at his job. I never actually heard him say a bad word about anyone.'

In the newsroom it was generally accepted that Richard's chief assets were that he was charming and even-tempered.

'We always thought he would do well, although perhaps not quite so well as he has,' says one of the reporters. 'It was strange, though. He didn't leave any great impression there. Once he'd gone, we all forgot him. It was like he'd never existed and that's strange for someone you've worked with for a year.'

But for Richard his time at Yorkshire was invaluable, not least because it was where he did his first interview with a Hollywood star. Gloria Swanson was doing a whistle-stop tour of Britain to promote her autobiography, *Swanson on Swanson*. Richard was given the plum job of interviewing her. From the moment he was given the assignment Richard, ever the professional, spent every waking moment doing his homework. He wanted to know every detail of the lady's life when he finally came face to face with her.

'He read that book from cover to cover,' remembers Lynda, 'and he discovered that one of her pet hates was men who lifted her hand to their mouth to kiss it. She was a tiny lady, you see, and it irritated the life out of her when men yanked her arm up towards their mouth instead of doing it in what she believed to be the correct way, by *bending down* to kiss her hand.'

So when Gloria Swanson swanned into the studio at Yorkshire, Richard knew exactly what to do. On being intro-duced to the star, who was by this time in her eighties, Richard looked her directly in the eye, gave her a captivating smile and bent down to kiss her hand.

'Well, that was it,' says Lynda. 'She fell in love with him on the spot. The interview went like a dream and afterwards she told Richard that if ever he was in Los Angeles, he had a standing invitation to come and visit.

'He came home that night on an absolute high. He'd achieved what he wanted to achieve by doing a faultless interview and he'd got an invitation to a Hollywood star's home into the bargain. I still have the Swanson video. I've never had the heart to tape over it because I know how much it meant to Richard. She was the ultimate for him at the time.'

But if his colleagues at Yorkshire did not see Richard in the role of current affairs reporter, he'd convinced his wife and friends at home that it was precisely what he wanted to do.

'He was very into politics and current events,' says Lynda. 'And he was always very interested in other people's views. He made it clear that he had no time for what he considered light subjects. He wasn't the least bit interested in everyday events and tittle-tattle which is why I find what he's doing now so astonishing.

'I don't watch *This Morning* very often but I did see a programme where Richard was presenting an item that involved road testing tights. I couldn't believe it. There was a procession of models who had to do various things wearing tights from all different hosiery companies. Then at the end Richard had to interview them as to how the tights had stood up to the strain and see whether or not they were laddered. I couldn't believe it! This was the man who used to make me tape him every night on TV so that he could examine his performance. He was sure he was going to be the next Robin Day and needed to know he was doing everything absolutely right.'

But, for all his high hopes of Yorkshire, the big career advance had not materialised. So when he was approached by Granada Television in 1982, Richard had no hesitation in accepting their offer. Mike Short, who had rejoined regional programmes as a producer in 1981, had been at Yorkshire Television on business when he spotted Richard.

'A few months later when one of the reporters on *Granada*

Reports left to go to London, I suggested they have a look at this young lad I'd met over in Yorkshire, whom I felt had the potential to be a presenter. Richard was approached and accepted immediately because he understood the opportunities Granada offered in terms of network.'

Lynda Madeley was thrilled about her husband's new job. What she didn't understand was that the move to Manchester was the beginning of the end for their marriage.

'In the beginning he came home every night and we made plans for the weekend when we'd both go house-hunting to Manchester in search of our new home. I loved him very much and I know he loved me.

'I remember him coming home one Friday evening. I was already in bed but he came bounding up the stairs, scooped me out and told me to close my eyes because he had a surprise. He led me downstairs in my nightie, opened the front door, and throwing his arms wide, pointed to something in the street: "Da-daaaaaaa!" And when I opened my eyes I saw he had bought a gleaming white Jaguar. He drove me around the country in the middle of the night in that car. He was so happy with it. We were both happy.'

But that was about to change.

It had been a wonderful summer. Richard was excited about his new job. Lynda was happy because Richard was finally doing what he wanted: working as a presenter. But one night in the November of that year he came home and said he had decided to find digs in Manchester during the week. He said that because the nights were drawing in and the weather was changing, the daily trip across the Pennines was becoming too dangerous. Lynda wasn't happy about it. She'd miss him. But she knew it made sense. She'd sleep easier knowing he was safe in Manchester.

Eventually Richard found a room in a house. But when Lynda asked where, he refused to tell her. 'He would never tell me where he was staying. He refused point blank to give me an address or telephone number. And when I said there was no way I could contact him if there was an emergency after working hours, he said that was OK because he'd phone me.

' "But don't worry," he said to me. "The landlady's fat, forty and ugly." '

A few months later Richard went home and told his wife their marriage was over.

'Everyone who knew us, everyone who socialised with us, could not believe it when they found out he had left me. They saw we were happy,' says Lynda. 'And that's what hurts. From the very beginning I had always told Richard that if he ever fell out of love with me, I wanted to know. I didn't want him looking for someone else while he was still with me.

'I had made him promise to tell me if ever he wanted someone else so that we could try and sort it out or so I could let him go. And I would have let him go because I loved him enough to do it.'

Lynda says wryly, 'Now that I'm older, I look back and see what was happening. Maybe I was stupid not to see the signs. Or maybe I did see them but I didn't want to admit he was seeing someone else.

'It was all very ironic because when he went to Manchester he told me he wanted to be the image of the perfect husband. He even told me he was avoiding eye contact with the women in the office because he didn't want to get into trouble.'

On 19 February 1983, Lynda Madeley was sitting in the cosy living room of their cottage in Aberford, waiting for her husband to get home. It was Friday and because he was due home from Manchester she had lit the coal fire in the tiny sitting room. Even if she said it herself the cottage *did* look beautiful. They'd only been in De-Laci Cottage a year or so but it had been time enough for Lynda to work her magic. She'd hung pretty chenille curtains at the windows and the antiques she'd been collecting since a young girl were scattered all over the house. She'd be sad to leave the tiny cottage that had been such a happy home for them. But since she'd been married to Richard, Lynda had taught herself not to become too attached to houses or places. With his job they would always be moving on.

Anyway, that night she was excited. For weeks she'd been trying to put some of their belongings into packing cases in readiness for the big move to Manchester and she was pleased with her progress. The cottage had finally been sold and Richard told her they had made a tidy profit. She didn't know how much because he always dealt with money matters. But however much it was, it would be a good down payment for their new home in Manchester. She and Richard had been house hunting there for months but still hadn't found anything they both liked.

Richard had suggested she go and stay with her mother in Cambridge until he found somewhere for them to live. Lynda had decided that once De-Laci Cottage was gone she was going to Manchester to be with her husband. They'd been apart too long. She'd live with him in a bedsit if she had to, but they'd have to do something quickly. They had to be out of the cottage in eleven days.

She heard the purr of the Jaguar outside the door. But the minute he walked in, Lynda could see something was wrong.

'Richard pulled up a couple of seats before the fire and calmly told me our marriage was over. I thought I hadn't heard him properly, then I looked into his eyes and knew I had. My mind was racing. This wasn't the way it was supposed to be. Why was he saying our marriage was over?

'At first I kept saying, "No, no, I won't accept this." I couldn't breathe. I just kept sobbing and sobbing and trying to catch my breath.'

As she sat gasping in shock, her husband pulled out a booklet entitled *Do Your Own Divorce*. He told her not to worry. He had talked to a friend at Granada who was a solicitor and been advised they could simplify things by handling it themselves.

It was like a nightmare; Lynda huddled before the cosy fire, her body racked by sobs, listening to the man she still loved telling her their marriage was over.

'I was trying to catch my breath and he was reading this booklet out and telling me the stages I would go through. "There are five key stages. First you'll feel shock and disbelief. Then there will be anger. After that will come bitterness and finally you will get to the stage of acceptance." He was so terribly matter of fact about it all.

'I was sobbing uncontrollably and he kept asking me where I wanted to live. He kept repeating, "Leeds, what about a bedsitter in Leeds? Or Harrogate. You've always liked Harrogate. Do you want to live in Harrogate?" I couldn't breathe, let alone tell him where I wanted to live. I just kept asking him what had happened. Why was he ending our marriage?

'I told him we needed time together in Manchester so we could sort everything out like we had always done. But he wouldn't hear of it. He just kept repeating, "No, it's all over." I was in a state of total shock. I'd never seen this hard-nosed side of Richard before. But when I looked into his eyes I saw his love for me had gone.'

That night Richard slept alone upstairs in the marital bed. Lynda lay downstairs on the couch, crying, trying to make sense of what had happened.

The next morning he was up bright and early. He told Lynda to get into the car because they were going to find her somewhere to live. 'I was like a zombie,' she says. 'I would have jumped off a bridge that day if he had told me to. I looked and felt dreadful. He drove me to Harrogate and bought a local paper which had flats to let in it. We spent the morning ringing landlords from telephone boxes. In the end I couldn't stand any more and told him to take me home.'

At the end of that day Richard Madeley walked out of his wife's life. Six years of marriage was over in less than 24 hours. 'He didn't hold me, he didn't hug me. He just told me there was some money from the sale of the house and I would get half.'

The only time she ever saw him after that was the day the removal van came to De-Laci Cottage. 'He pulled up in his car just as the van was driving away. All he said was, "I've come to get my things." That was it. Over.'

Thirteen years on, Lynda still has boxes of Richard's belongings. 'He left so suddenly that I still have the stuff I packed away thinking we were going into rented accommodation in Manchester. I have books belonging to his father, silver cups, his college scarf. His twenty-first birthday present from my mother.'

When Richard walked out on Lynda she had no money, and once the house was handed over to its new owner, nowhere to live. Eventually a member of her drama group offered her a room in his house.

She says now: 'I don't know what I feel about Richard any more. I've packed away whatever feelings I might have had for him in a box with my wedding dress. I don't hate him. I just wish he'd had the courage to come to me and say, "I'm having an affair." That way I would have understood why my marriage was over.

'Later he told me he didn't want me to name Judy as the third party in our divorce. He said he wanted it to be "irreconcilable differences" but I refused to do that on the grounds that it was a lie. He was protecting Judy's innocence all the way down the line. It didn't matter about me any more.

'And even after he left, everything was always about Judy. He kept pushing me for a divorce, saying the two of them wanted to start a family. I told him he didn't have to be married to start a family, and he said, "Judy and I want to do things properly." '

Lynda thinks that the fact Richard and Judy have children may have made him grow up a bit. 'Maybe he has changed. I suppose he must have because when I hear about this perfect husband who cooks and cleans, it's not the Richard I knew. The man I knew refused to lift a finger in the house and he couldn't boil an egg.

'In a way I feel sorry for Judy because I know what Richard is like. No one can keep pace with him. He is absolutely possessed by his work. He feeds on it. And I suspect she doesn't.'

Does she blame Judy for falling in love with her husband?

'If he told her he and I were having problems, it's not her fault. He was making himself available. So how can I say she broke up our marriage? And I don't hate him for leaving me. Maybe he didn't want to hurt me by telling me he was having an affair. I just don't know,' says Lynda.

It is clear that Lynda is still hurt and mystified by the break up with Richard. To her, it was a bolt from the blue, something inexplicable. From the outside, though, it would seem that the failure of the marriage is the classic story of one partner racing ahead professionally while the other, for the best possible reasons, merely stands still.

There is no doubt that all the time she was married to Richard, Lynda put her own needs, preferences and ambitions on hold. She contented herself with providing a stable home life for her husband. But at a time when he was forging ahead professionally, stability was probably not on his list of priorities.

When they married Richard was just 20, and Lynda a very young 27. The years between 20 and 30 can bring about a radical change in outlook; a character barely formed in its teenage years can mature in totally unexpected directions. Viewed in this light, perhaps the break up between Richard and Lynda was not really so surprising – though there is no denying the pain and the sense of betrayal it caused.

Today Lynda Madeley lives in an old farmhouse in Wensleydale with the new man in her life. She is three months younger than Judy Finnigan and the years have been kind to her. She has a mane of glossy red hair, a toothpaste-ad smile and she is a trim size 10. But, much more importantly, she has become her own woman.

'I will never forget that I was once married to Richard but it's time for the newspapers to stop hounding me every time he does something that is deemed to be newsworthy. Half the things I'm supposed to have said, I haven't. And I'm tired of being known as the jealous bitch who was left behind, who spends her time slagging off her ex-husband and the wife who replaced her. I have a ten-year-old daughter and I don't want her being chased by newspapers because her mother was once married to Richard Madeley.'

There is an argument that if Lynda Madeley had never said anything at all in the press about her relationship with Richard, the newspapers might have left her alone – although that seems a little unlikely as some were actually offering £1,000 in a village pub a few miles away from where she lives to anyone who would tell them her address.

There is little doubt that newspapers have pestered Lynda, but her reasons for speaking to them are still unclear. Did she do it because she believed the journalists when they said if she told the whole story of her life with Richard they would leave her alone for good? Or was there an element of revenge in her regaling the public with the inside story? Did she look at him with his glamorous wife and seemingly perfect marriage and wonder why it couldn't have been her?

Lynda says that, even though she is now happily living with the new man in her life, she will *never* marry again.

4 Falling in Love

WHEN JUDY FINNIGAN first clapped eyes on the man who was to shake her life to its foundations, he was nervously pacing the corridors of Granada Television. It was 1982 and it was Richard Madeley's first day as a presenter on Granada's nightly magazine programme, *Granada Reports*. Would he be able to make the grade? He had worked so hard on acquiring interview technique and a likeable screen persona, and of course his clean-cut good looks had done him no harm. Tall and impossibly slim, he always dressed for work in smart, conservative suits.

It is part of a TV presenter's stock in trade to be hyper-aware not just of their clothes but of their whole appearance. Richard knew how his face moved on screen; how his hair flopped on to his forehead if he moved too quickly. He knew how to smile just enough so his eyes didn't crinkle too much at the corners – and he also knew that those eyes could be used to great advantage. Lis Howell, his friend at Border Television, had told him that. She'd laughed and said he looked like a lounge lizard when he was talking to women. His greatest strength on screen was that women liked him and men didn't find him threatening. There wasn't an inch of Richard's screen persona he hadn't honed and polished to perfection but on that first morning, pacing the corridors of Granada, his usual confidence had deserted him.

Granada had a formidable reputation as a powerhouse of talent, a company that liked to employ promising people not for what they were but for what they might become. For Richard Madeley this was the biggest challenge of his career and it scared him. It had been easy to shine at Radio Cumbria.

Even at Border Television and then Yorkshire he was still perfecting a skill he hoped would take him to the dizzy heights of prime time. And now here he was at Granada. This could be his introduction to the big time.

'Hello,' he heard a calm, reassuring voice say behind him. Richard only realised the gentle, honeyed voice was talking to him when a soft white hand came to rest on his shoulder. Slowly he turned around and for a few seconds found himself trapped in the gaze of the most piercing blue eyes he had ever seen. 'I'm your mummy,' said the voice which, when Richard had recovered from the bolt of electricity that passed through him, he saw belonged to one of the most gorgeous women he had ever met.

Judy Finnigan was also a presenter on *Granada Reports*. She was 33 years old. She had a shock of flaxen hair, dazzling blue eyes, cheekbones as high as the Empire State Building, and a body that any man would have found sexy. She wasn't classically beautiful but she exuded sensuality from every pore.

In those days at Granada, when a new person started work he or she was assigned a minder or 'mummy', to familiarise him or her with the new workplace. 'Mummy' had to tell newcomers where the loo and canteen were, where they could find the stationery, and, more to the point, who was and who wasn't important in the office.

When everyone in the newsroom heard that Granada had taken on a good-looking 26 year old to co-present the programme, Judy and the other presenters were keen to find out everything there was to know about this new kid on the block. He was young. He had to be good otherwise Granada wouldn't have taken him on. But just how good was he? Would he be better than them? Was he after their jobs? It was all a bit unsettling so Judy decided to do a spot of investigating. She called one of her friends at Yorkshire to see what she could dig up. A few minutes later she walked back into the newsroom, giggling like a schoolgirl.

'They call him "the mannequin",' she said.

Richard Madeley's suits were pressed to perfection. His shirts had never seen a hint of a crease. He never had a hair out of place. He was the model of self-restraint. He never drank too much. Never smoked too much. He never shouted in the newsroom and on screen had the unnerving ability to stay cool whatever the crisis. He was controlled and in control. With Richard things didn't just happen, they went according to plan.

He was already carving out for himself a reputation as a first-rate presenter. 'He was a good presenter and later on he had an excellent career as a games show host,' says a producer who worked with him at the time. 'Granada did about four series of a game show called *Runway* and Richard impressed us all. Sometimes they would record up to four shows a day and Richard was the one at the end of the fourth recording who could still remember the round scores from the first show. He had a remarkable memory.'

'Richard can *do* it. He was also good fun,' remembers Mike Short, a former producer on *Granada Reports*. 'He'd send really rude messages around the system. I'd be sitting there talking to some big boss and this horribly rude message would come up on screen. I'd be trying to wipe it off so the boss couldn't see it. Richard took the mickey out of people then. He was fun.'

Slowly, behind the scenes, a relationship between him and Judy began to develop. They were already a couple on screen. Rod Caird, the editor of *Granada Reports*, had decided that this newest recruit would look good alongside Granada's golden girl. The pairing proved an unqualified success, on screen and off it.

But even though it was obvious what was going on with Richard and Judy, there were still many people at Granada who couldn't understand the attraction. 'Maybe he was fantastic in bed or something,' says an old female friend of Judy's who worked at the television centre. 'But we all suspected the biggest attraction for her was his age. He was very smooth and very persuasive and it must have been nice for her to have a much younger man chasing her around. I think most of us thought it would just be a flash in the pan.'

One of the male on-screen reporters says: 'I think it was a control thing. In her relationship with David, Judy was probably the junior partner intellectually. With Richard, *she* was the brighter one, the older one, the more experienced one. He was totally besotted with her. A friend of mine once said that the perfect relationship between a man and a woman was one where the man was slightly more in love with the woman than she was with him. That would be my definition of Richard and Judy. Once he had been captured by Judy, Richard was under her spell. In his eyes she could do no wrong.'

And Richard was having an effect on Judy. Suddenly, the woman who had never been particularly ambitious became as fanatical about her work as Richard. The two of them would arrive at Granada's production offices every day before work and ask the girls to re-run the film of the previous night's programme. Says one of the producers who worked with them: 'Richard used to watch every single programme he ever did with a notebook in his hand, jotting down what he thought were his mistakes and what he thought he'd done well. Anyone else would have looked at a film of themselves and felt sick, or at the very least been a bit embarrassed, but not Richard. He even got Judy doing it in the end. She'd never bothered to look at tapes of herself before Richard came along. It would never have occurred to her. We were all amazed to see the change in her.'

That change in Judy was obvious to everyone who knew her. And what was even more obvious was the fact that she was becoming increasingly involved with the baby-faced presenter whom everyone had thought would be no more than a passing fancy. Judy no longer made jokes about 'the mannequin'. She spent less time with her friends and more with Richard, and she became endlessly fascinated by her work – especially if that work happened to involve Richard Madeley.

Although Richard and Judy were reporters as well as presenters, they rarely went 'out on the road' after they started presenting together. 'They were both terribly clear about their status,' says one producer. 'They wanted to be presenters and that was that.'

Colleagues would see them chatting together in quiet corners of the newsroom, their heads close together. For a while no one was sure exactly what was going on between them. Their chats in the office grew more and more intimate. They were flirty and always seemed to be having fun together. They'd gone from having nothing whatsoever to do with each other to having communal lunches with everyone in the office. But almost imperceptibly, the lunches with people in the office stopped, as did the drinks in the Stables Bar after work. If Richard and Judy went out to lunch, it was alone. Although at that stage there was never any real proof that they were having an affair, the office was rife with rumours. And there were plenty of clues: the knowing looks, the shared jokes, the intimacy that only comes when two people are a couple. But no one knew for sure.

Then one morning, one of *Granada Reports*' young researchers, rushed into the office to say he'd spotted Richard and Judy walking up Quay Street on their way to the Granada offices. They'd been holding hands and laughing. That was enough for most of the hacks who for months had been listening to them deny there was anything between them.

But there was more to come. Debbie Pollitt was one of the girls on the production team. She and Judy were friends. Debbie had been her producer on *Reports Action*. The dark-haired young producer lived in a large high-ceilinged flat in Didsbury's Parkfield Road South. It was a leafy, tree-lined avenue full of grand three-storey Victorian houses. Only the very rich could afford to live in the vast, imposing villas, but two had been converted into spacious flats and were rented out to the single professionals who colonised Didsbury in the eighties. In those days it was a Mecca for Manchester's young and successful. On a par with London's Chelsea, its busy bars were bursting with journalists, lawyers, doctors and architects. Its restaurants and cafes catered for Manchester's media and professional elite.

Because they were both still married and had nowhere to meet, Richard and Judy 'borrowed' a flat in one of the old stone houses. They spent whole nights there and it was after one such night that Debbie Pollitt accidentally stumbled on their secret. She had been out with friends the night before and was late for work. So instead of taking the bus as she usually did, she decided to grab a taxi outside her flat. Just as she was stepping inside the cab, she looked up and saw Richard and Judy coming out of the flat next door to hers, holding hands. She couldn't believe it at first and had to look again to make sure. It was them all right. They were stepping into Richard's very distinctive Jaguar that was parked outside.

Debbie couldn't wait to get to work. By lunchtime that day everyone in Granada knew about Richard and Judy's secret love nest. 'Debbie came into the canteen and told everyone,' says one of the girls from the production office. 'No one could have been expected to keep that kind of information secret. It was just confirmation of what we all knew and what they had spent months denying.'

Says a reporter in the newsroom at the time: 'You can imagine what happened after we heard that not only were they having an affair, they were actually using someone's flat. It went around the office like wildfire. Everyone was talking about it – at the coffee machines, in the canteen, out on the road. It was hot gossip.'

It is hard not to feel some sympathy for Richard and Judy at this time. Whatever the rights and wrongs of the situation, these were two people who were deeply in love but forced to mask their feelings for each other in the face of intense curiosity and gossip mongering from their closest colleagues, even their friends. It was an impossible situation and an angry Richard was publicly protective of Judy when the rumours flying around the office reached their ears. No doubt Judy must have wanted to protect her husband from finding out about Richard before she was certain of what she wanted and ready to tell David.

But even though Richard and Judy still tried to keep the lid on their relationship in public, there were times when their passion overcame them. 'I remember we had an office party at a great big country house in Cheshire,' says one of Judy's former producers. 'Suddenly I looked across the room and saw Richard and Judy snogging in the corner for all they were worth. I suddenly realised that everyone else was looking at them as well. No one actually said anything. We all just stood there, open mouthed, thinking, Bloody hell!'

Their affair deepened, and it wasn't long before her husband, David, realised that their marriage was disintegrating. He had previously been confronted at the family home at Fallowfield by two reporters from a Sunday tabloid who had got wind of Judy's infidelity and had turned up on the doorstep to question David. If the reporters had expected the gentlemanly David Henshaw to fly into a jealous rage or even display a hint of reproach about his wife's affair, they were disappointed.

'My wife is not here,' he told them politely. 'She'll be back a bit later. And if you have no further questions, gentlemen, I'll bid you goodnight.'

Determined to do everything in his power to save his crumbling marriage, David decided that he and Judy should throw a summer lunch party in the garden of their house in Fallowfield. The day of the party was glorious. Sun blazed down on to their pretty garden, ablaze with summer flowers.

The first guests started to arrive around noon and, whether it was the sun or the never-ending stream of drinks that were being served in the garden, everyone seemed to be in a frivolous mood. It was well known among their friends that David and Judy knew how to throw a good party. They weren't wild socialites but their dinner parties were always stimulating occasions. In those days they were part of the northern media elite, who counted among their friends some quite senior and powerful people in television. That particular Sunday, some of David's more 'serious' friends from the BBC had been invited, together with Judy's colourful pals from Granada.

And then Richard Madeley arrived, clutching his guitar and a bottle of wine. He'd been to David and Judy's house for dinner, though whether that was before or after he began his affair with Judy, no one quite knows for sure.

Lunch had been a great success. The food was good, conversation flowed as freely as the wine, and no one seemed to have the vaguest intention of going home. The afternoon wore lazily on. People talked and laughed and drank. No one wanted the day to end.

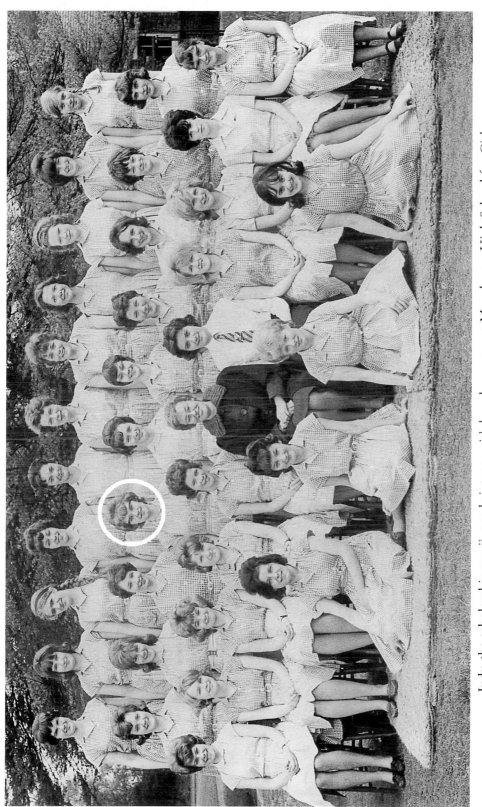

Judy, the scholarship pupil, aged sixteen, with her classmates at Manchester High School for Girls

The house where Judy lived – Birchfields Road, Manchester

Richard Madeley and Lynda Hooley on their wedding day, 31 July 1977

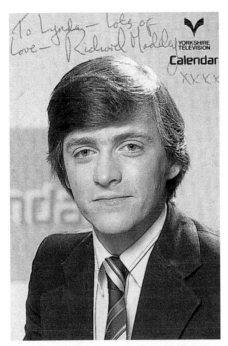

One of the many publicity cards Richard signed for his wife

On holiday, making the most of his torso

'He had a lovely soft voice, a bit like Al Stewart. He would always take his guitar and sing to whoever would listen' – Lynda Hooley, Richard's first wife

Meeting the locals while on holiday in the Gambia with his first wife, two months before he left her

'Fantasy woman' Linda Barker, Richard's landlady and lover

The early days of *This Morning* – TV's golden couple

Looking happy and relaxed, with one of the twins

Relief after Judge Sachs delivered a 'not guilty' verdict at Richard's trial, 4 July 1991

A rare night out

Richard and Judy
celebrate five years
of *This Morning*,
Britain's most
popular morning
programme

The *This Morning* team

Before the move from Manchester. What will the
future in London hold?

Judy looked radiant. She was wearing a floaty summer dress, and as she chatted and laughed with her guests she seemed to come alive in front of them.

By early evening, people started to move inside the house. Then someone suggested that Richard should play his guitar. Always glad of an opportunity to play, he perched himself on one of the chairs in the sitting room. Judy sat opposite, David somewhere in the middle of the room. As Richard started to play, it soon became abundantly clear to everyone in the room that he was serenading Judy. The more he sang, the more she fixed her eyes on him.

'It was incredible,' says one of the guests. 'We'd all had a lot to drink by that time. Judy was sitting with her feet up on a chair, and as Richard played her skirt slid higher up her bare legs. Nothing was said but it was obvious that something was going on between them.'

And all the while David Henshaw sat in the middle, watching. He was a spectator to the disintegration of his own marriage and there was absolutely nothing he could do about it.

'Someone else might have smacked Richard and told him to get out,' says the guest. 'But even though he must have been dying inside, David kept his cool and said nothing. He remained civilised to the end.'

It wasn't long after that party that Judy admitted to David she was in love with Richard. She told him there was no point in trying to save their marriage – it was over. What she felt for Richard was too strong. She had to be free to pursue it.

Judy Finnigan hadn't ended her marriage lightly. She had been worried about their twin sons and how they would cope, living apart from their father. 'She was very concerned about the effect it might have on the boys and how it would be done,' says one of Judy's co-presenters on *Granada Reports*. But Richard represented something that she wanted made permanent. There could be no going back. A few weeks later she asked David to vacate the marital home. She was going to keep the children.

'David left the house,' says a close friend of the couple. 'I don't think at that stage she wanted him to fight for her,' says another. 'But even if he had, it wouldn't have made any difference. She was madly in love with Richard.'

At the time of the break up, David was working on a programme for *Brass Tacks*. He was making a documentary about the *Daily Star* newspaper, whose headquarters were then in Manchester. The idea was to make a film that looked at a week in the life of a tabloid newspaper. The cameras would follow the reporters out on the road to see how they tackled stories. But, try as he might, David couldn't concentrate on his work. He had done as his wife asked and moved out of the marital home into a tiny bachelor flat in Manchester. He was trying to get on with his life. But he was hurt, unhappy, and terrified he was going to lose his children.

He was almost resigned to the fact that Tom and Dan would live with Judy, and though in his heart he knew it was the only practical solution, it still hurt. David's job meant he was likely to have to dash off anywhere at any time. He couldn't look after two young boys on his own. Sole custody for him was never really an option.

'Even if I had wanted to take them on full time it just wouldn't have been practical,' says David. 'My job involved being away for more than half the year. But I did believe that joint custody would work, regardless of where the boys lived. So, because I was working in Manchester at the time, the boys were able to spend a lot of time with me – most weekends in fact. It was an arrangement which suited me very well.'

David Hudson, a reporter on the *Daily Star* who was working with David on his film, says the whole business was very hard for David. 'It would have been hard for any father. He had lost his wife. He didn't want to lose his children as well. He doted on those boys, talked about them the whole time. The idea of losing them to Richard was tearing him apart.'

David spent a lot of time with his new-found friends at the *Daily Star*. He went out on the road filming with them. He drank with them after work in the Land O Cakes pub, which was just across the road from the Black Lubianka in Great Ancoats Street. He was comfortable among these friendly hacks who took his mind off what was happening. He liked their jokes, their banter, and the constant mickey taking about him being a BBC 'star'. All the reporters on the paper knew what had happened between him and Judy but he was one of their own. No one asked any intrusive questions.

Today David has found new happiness with his second wife, Lesley, whom he married in 1992. The couple have a young son.

5 Heartbreak

DAVID HENSHAW WASN'T the only person to be hurt by Richard and Judy's affair. There was someone else.

Linda Barker was a secretary in the typing pool at Granada when she first met Richard Madeley. It was November 1982 and the production crew lads from local programming were frantically trying to put together a scratch band for the 'locals' Christmas party. This bash had the reputation of being the best party of the festive season. *Everyone* wanted to go. It wasn't like some of the others where you had to sip wine, nibble crisps and make polite conversation with the heads of department. The locals party went with a swing, which is why tickets were sold out weeks in advance.

It had been decided that year that Linda Barker would be the singer to front the band on the night of the big party. She was the obvious choice with her pink and blonde punk hairstyle and her skin-tight skimpy dresses which had the men gasping for breath as she sashayed through the office every morning. Linda looked raunchy. She was exactly the sort of extrovert who could carry off lead vocals in a rock band.

Which was incredible considering that, just a few months before, she could never have passed for a rock singer. She'd had dull, mousy hair, wore big, dowdy clothes, and she was shy. And having spent a lifetime trying to lose weight, Linda still clocked in at 11½ stone. It would have been fine if she'd been 5ft 10ins. But she was 5ft 5ins. There was no getting around it – Linda was big. Her metamorphosis from frump to fantasy woman had been a process her friends at work witnessed in awe and amazement.

For as long as anyone could remember Linda had always

been a 'big girl'. But it was her face, with its saucer-sized grey-green eyes, her quick smile and smooth, white skin that drew people to her. Linda was pretty, but because of her weight she lacked confidence, even though Linda herself suspected it was lurking somewhere just beneath the surface. She knew that inside that frumpy body was a wonderful, wacky girl waiting to get out. Of course she wanted to be thin. She wanted to be able to buy skin-tight jeans, itsy-bitsy skirts and sexy black stockings like all the rest of her friends. That was why she had spent most of her adult life ricocheting from one crash diet to another.

But neither life nor her weighing scales had been kind to Linda. Every Monday she would excitedly tell the girls in the office that she was starting some new 'miracle' diet. Every Tuesday she would dejectedly tell them she'd try again next week. It seemed there was always some conspiracy to stop her losing weight. Her two main problems were that she was doing a job that wasn't challenging enough and she was locked in a long-term relationship that was going nowhere. With work problems and man trouble, what hope did she ever have of losing weight?

Ironically, it was 'man trouble' that finally helped Linda shed not just three stone but her frumpy image and all her inhibitions as well.

Initially she had been devastated when the seven-year relationship with someone she had loved very much ended suddenly and traumatically. Her head told her it was the best thing that could have happened because living with her boyfriend just hadn't worked. But when it finally ended, that didn't stop her heavy heart from feeling as if it were breaking. Linda couldn't eat, she couldn't sleep, she couldn't even think straight.

Then, one day, she looked in the mirror and she couldn't believe what she saw.

For the first time in her life she had cheekbones. More than that, she had hip bones *and* a waist. It had been weeks since the split from her ex and the young secretary had been so devastated she had simply forgotten to eat. All the years of failed diets, the self-doubt – and here she was looking exactly how she'd always wanted to.

As Linda began to realise that she looked sensational, she stopped worrying about the man she'd lost and started thinking about all the men she might meet in the future. Because, looking like she did now, she knew it wouldn't be long before they were knocking her door down.

Almost overnight Linda changed. She had her long mousy hair cut and dyed white-blonde. She consigned everything that was baggy or had an elasticated waist to the bin and replaced them with slinky little numbers. Punk was in fashion and Linda decided she was going to make the most of it.

'The people in the office never quite knew what I was going to turn up in from one day to the next,' she says. 'In the beginning they had to look twice to see if it was really me. I wanted to look as different and as glam as I could. Because, for the first time in my life, I actually *liked* the way I looked.'

It was about four weeks before the Christmas party and people were just getting used to the new-look Linda. A group of musicians had finally been put together for the scratch band but there was still a lot of work to be done in rehearsals before they could actually call themselves a band. Linda had casually asked one day who the band's guitarist was going to be. She was told it was some new presenter from *Granada Reports* famous for his sharp suits and immaculate shirts. Great, thought Linda. Just the kind of guy we need in a rock band.

And so it was, on a chilly November night in one of the big old rehearsal rooms in Granada's Quay Street offices, that she came face to face for the first time with Richard Madeley.

'I'd never met him. All I'd heard was people talking round the office because he was always so immaculate. And that was exactly my reaction the first night I clapped eyes on him in rehearsals. I remember him being very sure of himself and what he wanted. But, to be honest, he didn't really register much with me then. All I could think about was being in the band.

'It was great fun because we got to pick our own songs. And it was exciting for me because for the first time in my life I was going to be able to show off – and, what's more, I knew I was going to look damn good while I was doing it.'

Linda had opted to sing a Frank Zappa number, which was

quite raunchy, and another called 'Pizza Man'. I purposely chose songs I thought no one else would know so that people wouldn't be able to tell if I was making a mess of them,' she says. As rehearsals got under way in earnest, Richard and Linda found themselves spending more and more time together.

Richard was drawn to the pretty young secretary who, for some reason, seemed to be grabbing life by the throat and shaking it for all she was worth. He didn't know then that she was making up for all the lost years. He might not have been so taken by the dowdy girl of a few months before. But this new Linda, who was positively bursting with life and throwing herself around on stage to the strains of Frank Zappa, was someone he definitely wanted to get to know better.

They became friends during pub sessions after rehearsals. Richard had told Linda he was married but that his wife was still living in Leeds and wouldn't be moving over to Manchester until he was sure how long he was staying at Granada. He'd hinted that there were problems in the marriage but at that stage didn't go into more detail. It was during one of these conversations that he happened to mention that he was looking for digs. He told Linda that the journey across the Pennines each day was growing more and more hazardous as winter took a grip. He wanted somewhere to stay during the week.

For Linda it seemed the perfect solution. Now that her ex had moved out she was looking for a lodger to help pay the mortgage on her three-bedroomed semi in Chorlton-cum-Hardy. On a secretary's wages she couldn't afford to keep the place on her own and Richard seemed like a nice bloke. She didn't fancy him or anything. And anyway, she didn't need any complications in her life just yet.

Linda had rented the front room out before. Even when she was living with her ex-boyfriend, the room had been perfect as a temporary stopping-off point for the armies of actors and film crews that were always passing through Granada. It was exactly what Richard was looking for, fed up with the daily trips from Leeds, and Linda was under no illusions about the arrangement.

'He was going to be my lodger, nothing more. I had a room

to rent and he gave me the impression he was desperate to get away from his wife.'

Richard moved into Linda's house on a Monday evening at the end of November. His classic Jaguar, packed from floor to ceiling with bulging suitcases, pulled up outside her front door just after 8pm. Linda was having a glass of wine in front of the fire when her new lodger arrived. She showed Richard to his room at the front of the house.

It was nice enough, if a little sterile. It had blue wallpaper and curtains and fitted wardrobes which Richard would need to house his vast collection of clothes. There was a tiny boxed-in fireplace and a small radiator. Linda left him alone to unpack while she went downstairs to pour a welcoming glass of wine.

It was getting quite late and Linda had to go to work the next day. She decided that after she'd had a quick chat with Richard and filled him in on the house rules, she'd go to bed. She poured herself another glass of wine and waited for him to join her. Suddenly she became aware that he was already there, framed in the doorway, wearing a green safari suit.

'I thought it was an odd thing to put on at the end of a day in the office,' she says. 'But then I realised Richard hadn't put it on to relax, he'd come to ask me what I thought he looked like in it. I have to admit, I was a bit stunned at first. This man hadn't been in my house an hour and it was obvious he was going to put on a fashion show for me.

'Everything he'd brought in those suitcases was whipped out and paraded in front of me,' says Linda. 'He wanted to know which clothes he looked best in. He seemed to want my genuine opinion of his clothes so I did my best to give it to him. I've been called "crazy" and "off the wall" in my time so I just thought, Well, if this is the way he enjoys life, who am I to argue?

'I couldn't believe the amount of stuff he kept in the bathroom either. There was so much of his hairspray there was hardly room for my things.'

In fairness to Richard, he isn't the only male presenter who uses cosmetics to enhance his on-screen appearance. Television lights are harsh and unforgiving and even radiantly healthy people can look wan and washed out beneath their glare. Bronzer to give the skin a glow, a discreet touch of mascara to widen the eyes and powder to counteract the skin's natural shine are par for the course. But Richard being Richard obviously liked to experiment with a whole range of products.

He did prefer a natural tan whenever possible and was typically thorough and methodical in the way he went about it.

'I remember coming home from work one day,' Linda says. 'It was beautiful outside and for some reason Richard was on holiday. I walked into the sitting room and saw that the French windows leading out on to my tiny garden were wide open.

'When I got out there, I couldn't believe what I saw. There was about two feet of available space in one sunny corner because the rest was taken up by a huge pile of bricks from an old outhouse that had been pulled down. And there was a bare-chested Richard, scrunched into the corner, arms outstretched, face to the sun, trying for all he was worth to get a suntan.'

For the first few weeks their relationship remained platonic. When Richard arrived back at night they'd often have a friendly chat over a glass of wine. If Linda wasn't around, they'd catch up when they could. When their affair began it was in a gentle, unhurried way. It certainly wasn't love at first sight for Linda. There were no thunderbolts, no racing pulses. But the man who looked as if he'd just stepped out of Burton's window was definitely starting to grow on her.

About three weeks after he had moved into the house Richard rang Linda at work and asked if she'd like to go and see the film *E.T.* that night. 'I suppose I should have been suspicious about his motives then. He told me we were going to have to go to Rochdale, which was more than fifteen miles away, to see the movie because everywhere else was booked up. Of course, it was because no one would see us so far from home.'

The two of them left the cinema in high spirits. The film had been a good old-fashioned tear-jerker and on the way home they decided there should *definitely* be more movies like it. By the time Richard's Jaguar pulled up outside Linda's house they were both ready for a drink in front of the roaring coal fire. Whether it was the wine, or just the culmination of the attraction that had been growing between them, the TV presenter put down his glass and slowly leant over to kiss Linda. She did not push him away. The affair had begun . . .

'I was very cross with myself next day,' remembers Linda. 'I had actually fought the attraction for weeks. Richard had tried to kiss me before but I'd always made it clear I was his landlady and I didn't want anything more complicated than that. Richard had been very good about it. He'd tried it on and it hadn't worked but there were no hard feelings. We even joked about it. But it didn't put him off. He kept trying until I eventually gave in.

'I suppose the reason I eventually let him make love to me in the end was because I'd just come out of a long-term relationship which ended badly and had sapped all my self-respect. I was vulnerable and saw that Richard really liked me. And if you don't have much confidence, and someone makes a big thing of liking you, then you like them back. I'd been in a relationship for seven years and Richard was my first real affair after that. I just needed someone to show me I was still attractive.'

The affair became intense very quickly. 'It was a very physical relationship,' says Linda. 'Richard was a good lover – at least in my terms he was. He was gentle and caring and totally unselfish in bed. And, yes, I suppose he was very interested in sex. But so was I. The passion was new and powerful. That's how it always is at the start of a relationship.'

Linda says that although she and Richard shared the same bedroom every night, he was adamant that their affair should be conducted in secret. 'I didn't want to know too much about his wife but he told me there had been a big problem with the age gap and that the relationship was finished. I believed at this stage that their marriage was over. He told me that, to all intents and purposes, he was a single man – and I believed him because he had moved so much of his stuff into my house.'

* * *

The Christmas party at Manchester's Placemates nightclub had been a rip-roaring success. Linda, with her two-tone hair, her skin-tight black leotard, black fishnet stockings and multi-coloured mini skirt, had been a sensation. After she'd belted out her numbers everyone had rushed to hug and kiss her and tell her how wonderful she'd been – everyone, that is, except the man who was sharing her bed. Richard kept away from Linda that night so as not to arouse suspicion among his colleagues.

He'd done his bit at the party, playing the Yamaha guitar which his wife had bought him for a 21st birthday present. He'd even decided a couple of weeks before that he would sing a few songs and so Lynda Madeley had spent a whole day sitting by the stereo at their home in Leeds and painstakingly writing down the lyrics of her husband's favourite Eagles songs. Lynda had been looking forward to meeting some of Richard's colleagues at the Granada Christmas party, but when she'd asked him what sort of dress she should buy, she was told she wasn't allowed to go. The party was just for staff, said Richard.

He was leading a double life. He was telling his wife that it wouldn't be long before she could join him in Manchester, and he was telling his mistress that they had to be on guard at all times because his wife didn't trust him and everything was getting very unpleasant.

'I was prepared to go along with it because I really liked him,' says Linda. 'For a while I even imagined I might be in love with him. I'd been hurt very badly in my previous relationship but Richard was so sensitive and caring with me. When I met him I had no self-respect and he restored that for me. I'd been fat for years and for the first time in as long as I could remember someone was putting in a great deal of effort to make me feel good about myself. I felt he was genuine. I think he was for a time.'

Richard even went to visit her when she was admitted to hospital with a gynaecological problem. 'He was there at my bedside when I came round from the operation. He picked me up, took me home and looked after me. No one had cared for me like that or been so tender in years.'

A couple of weeks before Christmas, Richard told Linda he was going on holiday to the Gambia. He told her he had booked it before he met her, but he promised to write, and he did, almost every day.

'He wrote me some of the most amazingly passionate love letters I've had in my entire life,' says Linda. 'They were very beautiful and I was totally overwhelmed by them. They were very romantic, and it was in those letters that he told me for the first time that he loved me.'

Meanwhile Richard, actually on holiday with his wife, was making a last-ditch attempt to mend his marriage. Linda Barker was back home in Manchester, blissfully unaware of what was going on. All she knew was that since Richard had gone on holiday there had been a stream of tender, passionate letters which she read and re-read until she knew them by heart. It was those letters that finally convinced Linda she was falling in love. And for the first time in years she was happy.

The only cloud on her horizon was that she couldn't share that happiness with anyone. Richard had forbidden it. Everything was going so well but she couldn't discuss the relationship with her friends or talk about it to the girls in the office because Richard would have gone crazy. Even when she was under pressure from girls in the typing pool, many of whom were convinced that something was going on between her and her handsome lodger, Linda knew she had to keep her mouth shut. Although, if truth be told, she didn't *really* understand the reasons why. Richard had said the secrecy was because he wanted to protect her from a messy divorce case. But how exactly was his wife going to find out? She was in Leeds after all. As for the people in the office, Linda knew they wouldn't care. Yes, there'd be a bit of gossip when they first found out, but after the initial shock no one would give a damn, she was sure of that.

What Linda didn't know was that there was one person who would have cared very much about her affair with Richard Madeley – a woman who was already beginning to fall in love with him herself.

Richard returned from the Gambia and everything seemed

fine for a while. Linda pretended not to care that he never took her out anywhere; that this love of theirs had to be kept so deeply under wraps.

'Because our affair was such a deep, dark secret we could never be seen out in public together. I must have been the cheapest date ever. We never went to a pub or a wine bar because people might have recognised us. In fact, the only time we ever went out for a meal together was when we split up, and even that was only for a lunchtime snack in a hamburger joint.

'His excuse was always that he didn't want to give his wife any reason to accuse him of having an adulterous affair, which was crazy because he *was* having an adulterous affair. But at the time I thought it made sense. He convinced me that all the cloak and dagger stuff was to protect me, to stop me from getting tangled up in a messy divorce.'

Richard and Linda had to be seen to be living separate lives. So when they bumped into each other in the corridors of Granada, Richard's instructions were that they were not to react to each other. They must not seem to be too friendly. There were to be no knowing smiles, none of the coy intimacy that lovers share. To the outside world Richard was a lodger and Linda his landlady.

'Even though we were working in the same building he wouldn't talk to me. He would say "Hello" if we passed in the corridor but he would never stop for a chat. Nor would he talk to me if we were both in the Stables Bar, which was Granada's pub on the premises. We were rarely together in the evenings. That was part of the façade.

'I carried on going out with my friends, although he made it perfectly clear he didn't like me going out clubbing. He said the girls I went out with were seen as being "easy" and I'd get a bad name if I spent too much time with them. On those nights he'd be waiting up for me when I got home. And I suppose that was part of the excitement. It seemed dangerous, thrilling somehow, to be in a club or a wine bar, knowing that when I got home "my man" would be waiting for me.

'I know I was stupid not to realise it wouldn't last. But

remember, I'd had a disastrous relationship and along comes this handsome man who says he loves me and wants to look after me. It was a time of great change in my life. I found that people suddenly liked me and wanted to spend time with me. God, I even began to like myself. And then along comes Richard, this TV presenter who was a *somebody*, and tells me he loves me.'

Linda says that although she and Richard shared a bedroom most nights, they still managed to hide their relationship from their friends who came to the house. 'Richard still kept his clothes in his own room. And he always got dressed there in the mornings. He kept his make-up and all his bits and pieces in the bathroom alongside mine. But no one was suspicious about that.

'It was never really a cosy relationship. Looking back now I realise that. But he did cook, and we always had lots to talk about. That was part of the attraction for us both. We were able to talk to each other. I suppose the nicest times we ever had were at the weekends when the shutters were down as far as work was concerned and we didn't have to worry. We used to go out for walks or a drive in the country. They were the best times for us.'

It was some time after his return from the Gambia that Linda realised her relationship with Richard was changing. 'He became distant. He wasn't as tender with me. I suspected he had someone else but I didn't know for sure. Then one day he told me he was going on a long weekend to Amsterdam. And it was after that he came back and told me he was moving out.'

It didn't take long for Linda to discover she was being replaced by Judy Finnigan. 'A researcher came up to me in the newsroom a couple of weeks after Richard had left my house and asked me if I'd heard about him and Judy. This man always knew the office gossip and he couldn't wait to pass it on when he got a juicy bit. He took great delight in telling me that, not only had Richard told everyone about our affair, but that he and Judy were now an item too.

'I was gutted. I thought, How could he? I was so hurt because he had told me he was in love with me. We'd never actually got round to planning our future because it was early days and the relationship was still very young. But there had been a point when I felt it was going that way.'

'When Richard left Linda for Judy, she was devastated,' says Irene McGlashin, who used to work in Granada's production office. 'She was pretty but had no confidence and when Richard left her she was heartbroken.'

The day Richard moved out is one Linda says she will remember for as long as she lives. 'I think what hurt me most was the fact that he wouldn't talk about why it was over between us. He just said he was moving out and that was it. He couldn't tell me what had happened or why he was leaving. I'm the sort of person who needs a confrontation. And I needed to know why a man who a few weeks ago had said he loved me, suddenly didn't.'

But what almost destroyed Linda was that as soon as Richard had decided he was moving out he told everyone in the office about their relationship. The man who for months had insisted on total secrecy suddenly began talking about their affair to anyone who would listen. 'I felt like he made me a laughing stock. I'd stupidly played his game – denying it, denying it, all the time. Every time anyone asked me if there was anything going on between us, I'd say "Absolutely not". Then suddenly he told everyone – just like that.'

Linda knew she needed to try and put her life back together again, but it was hard. She went to work every day and tried to carry on as normal. By then everyone knew what had been going on.

'I know now it was never love, it was infatuation. But it felt like love at the time. And what hurt the most is that he never explained what had gone wrong between us. The girls in the office tried to be terribly supportive but a lot of the men were sniggering behind my back.'

Linda Barker was a classic Cinderella, looking for a handsome prince. The dramatic change in her appearance, something she refers to again and again, had led her to expect that everything else in her life was going to fall into place just as easily. After years of dissatisfaction with her appearance and her relationships, she had fixed one factor in the equation and thought the other would fall into place too.

Only life isn't like that. Richard's obvious reluctance to make any commitment to her was plain. But Linda could not or would not acknowledge it and so the shock of his departure came as a huge and painful shock to her.

A few days after he left the house, Richard rang Linda and asked if he could stop by and pick up a few things he had left behind. She told him then that when he came round she wanted to talk. Richard knew he had no choice.

'He had moved out of my house and my life and he'd never had the courage or the decency to tell me why,' she says.

He arranged to come to the house the following Sunday and they agreed to have a meal at a Canadian-style hamburger restaurant in Withington.

'I wasn't tearful,' sayd Linda. 'I just wanted some answers.'

Richard absolutely denied he was seeing Judy. 'He said it was all just vicious rumour and the real reason he was leaving me was because things between us had been moving too fast and he just wasn't ready for a relationship.

But Richard was about to get one of the biggest shocks of his life from the girl he'd thought would go quietly. 'While we were still sitting at the table I passed him a piece of paper on which I'd written down all the things that had annoyed and hurt me. Because he'd refused to talk to me about what went wrong, I wanted him to know how I felt. I wanted him to know just what I felt about him.'

As he read Linda's character assessment of him, Richard's jaw dropped.

'He couldn't believe it. I think he was genuinely shocked that anyone could think those things about him. I felt better afterwards though. I had been intensely angry because of the way I'd been treated. But after he'd read my letter, after I saw the look of horror on his face, I felt I'd taken my first step into Life Without Richard Madeley.'

6 Together At Last

LINDA BARKER SET ABOUT trying to rebuild her life. But it was hard. Watching Richard and Judy's faces staring out at her from the TV every night was bad enough. Having to see them in the flesh around the offices at Granada was torture. The one consolation Linda had was that at least she didn't see them every day. She was still in the typing pool, which meant that she moved around the building.

When Linda first applied to Granada in 1979 she had finished teacher training two years before. 'I'd qualified in 1977 but that was when the government started to make cutbacks in the teaching profession. I'd spent three years at college only to find there were no jobs.'

As a safety precaution she'd taken a secretarial course. But what she really wanted to do, she decided, was to work in TV. 'I lost count of the number of job applications I sent in to Granada. I applied for anything and everything. I knew I couldn't be a reporter or presenter but I wanted to be a researcher.'

For two years Linda had no luck. She did temping jobs around Manchester but Granada was the prize. Eventually friends persuaded her that the only way to 'get her foot in the door' was to work as a secretary so that when jobs came up she'd be there on the spot.

By September 1983 Linda had almost given up hope of getting out of the typing pool when, out of the blue, she was offered the job of production assistant in the Granada news-room. That meant she would be working in the same office as Richard and Judy.

Linda didn't know if she was up to that yet – Richard had

only moved out a few months before. It wasn't that she thought about him all the time or she wanted him back or anything, but she'd seen him and Judy around the building together a few times and it had been difficult for her. If she took the job in the newsroom it would mean she would have to see them every day; what's more, she would actually be working for them. She'd have to watch Judy having the kind of relationship with Richard that *she'd* wanted.

Linda wasn't sure she was strong enough. And a part of her worried that she had only been offered the job in the first place as part of the point scoring politics that go on in any office. People may well have imagined she'd be a thorn in Judy's side and decided to put her in there just to see what would happen. It was a situation guaranteed to make both women feel anxious and uptight. Was that what Linda really wanted? She was in two minds about whether to take the job, then she remembered all the years she'd wasted temping while waiting for an opportunity like this.

'I just thought, beggar it,' she says. 'What's past is past. I'd waited for this chance for a long time and I wasn't about to let Judy Finnigan or Richard Madeley get in the way. I owed it to myself to make a success of my life.'

In the beginning, landing the job as production assistant had been a dream come true for the former secretary. It was the best of both worlds as far as she was concerned. She'd always wanted to work in television and even though she'd only been a secretary for the last few years, she'd enjoyed working with the people at Granada. They were a fantastic bunch and she'd made some good mates. Now she'd be with them as an equal, thanks to her new job. On the other hand, she was still very new to it and there were lots of things she didn't know.

'My job was to type crew lists, chase up researchers and reporters, follow up stories, organise film crews and get them out on stories,' says Linda, 'and I loved it, every minute of it. I was really having to use my brain. Everyone had to work fast in the newsroom because *Granada Reports* went out five nights a week. And having a deadline was a new challenge for me.'

But Linda still felt that her presence in the busy newsroom

might be a problem for Judy. 'I thought I was going to have to be very careful,' she says. Linda could just about bear having to watch her ex and Judy canoodling all day and sending each other love notes, but she says she could feel Judy's anxiety because of her presence.

The first flare up came on Linda's second day in the newsroom.

Every night on *Granada Reports*, when we did the weather forecast, we used to have this little slot where we'd flash up on screen a child's drawing that coincided with whatever the forecast was for the next day. We used to get hundreds of drawings sent in from kids all over Manchester and some of them were incredibly good.

'Every morning one of my jobs was to sift through these drawings and choose the best and the most appropriate for that day's weather. On my second day in the job Judy came over to my desk waving two scrappy little bits of paper. I saw that they were black and white drawings that her twin boys had dashed off. She told me very curtly that I had to use them on that night's weather report. I didn't say anything. Not yes. Not no. It was only my second day on the job and I didn't want a screaming match with the star presenter. I just thanked her for the pictures and off she went.

'When I looked up I saw that the news editor, Chris Rybczinski, was looking furious. As soon as Judy had gone he hissed at me, "We're not using those." I said that of course we weren't. They had been scribbled on scruffy, badly creased pieces of paper and they were black and white, no good for us on screen because we always used colour. Anyway, at that stage we didn't even know what the weather would be like. I suppose I'd got the idea there might be trouble when Chris said to me after Judy had gone, "Don't worry, I'll back you on that." I didn't know exactly what he meant but I didn't have the time to worry about it then.'

Linda thought no more about the drawings and got on with the rest of her day. She had a mountain of things to do and the episode with Judy soon went out of her mind. But that evening, just as the final credits of *Granada Reports* had rolled, a furious

Judy stormed into the newsroom. 'There was this angry mum shouting that she had promised her boys that their drawings would be on the programme and what was she to tell them?' claims Linda. 'I couldn't tell her the truth so I tried to be diplomatic and say they weren't appropriate for that day's weather. "It doesn't matter," said Judy. "I told my kids their pictures were going to be on TV tonight. And they weren't." '

Linda tried to calm her down but the presenter refused to be pacified.

'After that Judy and I didn't speak unless we had to. If I had a message to give to her, I'd give it. I was polite but I certainly didn't grovel. We gave each other a wide berth for a few months but in the end she actually tried to be nice to me. I think she understood that I wasn't a person to mess with. She also realised that nothing she could do was going to rattle or sway me. In the end she really didn't bother me any more.'

It's hard to see how the situation Linda and Judy found themselves in could be anything but awkward, with Richard's former and current lover forced into close proximity. Surely any woman would feel threatened by such a position? It is to both Linda and Judy's eventual credit that after the initial awkwardness they were able to go on and work together.

By September 1983 Richard and Judy's affair was in full swing, although they were still trying to deny that anything was going on. 'I remember that one day I had to go to the second-floor graphics department to deliver something,' says Linda. 'And just to make things interesting I decided to go a different route. Anyway, this particular day the route I chose was down the back staircase, and who should I bump into on the stairs but Richard and Judy in a passionate clinch. How on earth they imagined no one would see them I don't know.'

Rachel Purnell, who was a reporter in the newsroom when the affair began, says, 'From the minute they got together that was it. They were inseparable. They never operated as different entities after they fell in love. It was like they merged and became one person. They came to work together. They had lunch together. They were one. People used to say they were like a mirror image. They liked the things they saw reflected in one another.

By the mid eighties Richard and Judy had become the star presenters of *Granada Reports*. It had happened almost by accident. The evening magazine show was famed for reinventing itself. There was so much talent and so many ideas around that the show and its format were constantly changing. It was during one of these changes that Richard and Judy suddenly found they had landed the top jobs.

Tony Wilson, a businessman who founded Factory Records and the Hacienda nightclub in Manchester, has worked for Granada for 22 years and is still presenting the region's nightly magazine show, now called *Granada Tonight*.

'Richard and Judy are the ultimate TV pros,' he says. 'They are the kind of presenters who enjoy it when everything starts falling apart because that is when they are at their very best. They love it when a film breaks down because it means they can ad lib their way out of it and smooth everything over.

'I remember one night during the early eighties I had been held up on a story. For the first time in my career it meant I was going to be late for the sixty-second 'promo' which flagged the programme and told viewers what was coming up on that night's show.

'I was presenting the show that night with Richard and Judy but I was still in make-up when the promo went out on air. Needless to say I never made it, but Richard and Judy did the whole thing so beautifully without me that no one even realised I was missing.'

By 1984 Richard and Judy's relationship was a well-established fact of life in the Granada newsroom. 'In Judy, Richard saw everything he ever wanted,' says one of the executives of *Granada Reports*. One of its presenters, who worked alongside Richard and Judy, agrees. 'I think he [Richard] was bossed around by Judy, but I think that's what he wants from a woman. Judy is very strong and I think he needed that.'

There were many who believed that Richard was so in love with Judy that he put his career on hold for her. The man who had always been consummately ambitious and had never stayed in the same place for long, seemed content to stand still in career terms because of his feelings for Judy. Everyone kept telling him he was good enough to go to London, that there was no one his age who was such a good all-rounder. And it was true. But Richard knew that if he went south he might lose the woman he loved, and he wasn't prepared to chance that. Because for all his self-assurance, Richard was powerless in the face of his feelings for his co-presenter.

The man who had never lifted a finger in the house while he was living with his first wife suddenly realised he was going to have to change if he was to have a future with this intelligent, opinionated career woman and mother. He knew he would never again be the 'boss' as he was in his marriage to Lynda Hooley. She had allowed herself to always put her husband and his career first. Life with Judy Finnigan was going to be an entirely different proposition. She was too clever, too wordly, to be at any man's beck and call. Despite her protestations that she had never been ambitious, Judy managed to transform herself from a chubby, bespectacled researcher with no journalistic training into one of the region's top presenters.

But even if, as the stories go, Richard does most of the household chores, there are few who would deny the sexual chemistry that, after many years, still exists between them. They touch each other constantly; they reach out to take each other's hand the moment the *This Morning* cameras stop rolling. If they are having a drink in the editor's office after the programme they stand with their arms wrapped round one another. Even on a casual stroll round the dock, they behave like boyfriend and girlfriend.

'The sexual attraction is totally mutual,' says a former presenter of *This Morning*. 'The couple work together all the time, yet they are forever going away on "little honeymoons" without the children. Yes, they sometimes snap at each other in the studio but they are still very tactile. I would say Richard has always been the one who is openly besotted but there was always a great deal of possessiveness on Judy's side.'

A producer who has worked with the couple for the past ten

years says: 'If your wife behaves as though every woman is after you, then maybe you start to believe it's true. I think Judy knows she's in control but only to the extent that she's the intellectual master. The relationship is a curious combination of her bolstering him and putting him down.

'When she is challenged by Richard on screen she's quite canny about how she puts him down. She still does it but she is careful not to challenge him too vigorously.'

Besides being a passionate one, the relationship seems to be very insular too. Richard and Judy are both obsessive and possessive about each other and together they have created a nest that very few besides their children are allowed to enter.

So protective are they of their privacy that Judy refuses to have a full-time nanny living in their Manchester house. With their hectic schedule it would make sense to have someone on hand at all times to look after the children, but Judy will not suffer the intrusion of a 'stranger' living in their home. 'The minute Richard and Judy walk through the door at night, the daytime nanny walks out,' says a friend on *This Morning*. They could easily afford to have someone there full-time but they don't want anyone in the house.

Nest or 'prison', to quote Richard. He admitted in an interview with the *Daily Telegraph*'s Lynn Barber that the enforced closeness *was* difficult in those early days. 'We didn't have any news to exchange. But we've grown used to it now. We don't feel we are rubbing each other up at all.'

Richard and Judy were finally married on 21 November 1986 at Manchester Register Office. The wedding was a low-key affair because the couple were broke – so broke that they'd had to take out a £300 bank loan to pay for it. And although they had finally found personal happiness with one another, the previous two years had been fraught with difficulties.

Judy's father, John Finnigan, to whom she had always remained close, had died of cancer after a long and painful illness. His only daughter had been devastated by his death but after it she realised she could finally fully commit herself to Richard.

Although they had been living together for two years, so far Judy hadn't quite got her head around the idea of marriage. Tom and Dan were just seven years old and she didn't want to rush into anything that would affect them. And Richard was eight years younger than her. Statistically the chances were against a successful union. And there were those two failed marriages behind them . . .

It was her father's tragic death which finally tipped the balance for her. Judy was devastated when she discovered that John Finnigan had cancer. It seemed so cruel to her that a man who had worked hard for his family all his life was to be cheated out of time for himself at the end of it.

'It was a horrible time,' remembers Judy. 'I spent almost every minute of my time nursing Dad because my mother was nearly seventy. And because I had to spend so much time with Dad, I had to leave Tom and Dan with Richard. They got on like a house on fire and that's what made me realise what a fantastic father Richard would make.'

Given the depth of the love and closeness between Richard and his own father, that is perhaps hardly surprising.

Richard and Judy could only afford a week in the Cotswolds for their honeymoon but it didn't matter. They had the rest of their lives for lavish holidays. For now, all that was important was their love for each other – and the baby Judy was expecting. Says Judy: 'I remember telling Richard it felt physically different being married. What I didn't know was that I *was* different – I was pregnant.'

The couple were ecstatic. Judy was 37 then and knew if she was going to have Richard's babies they didn't have time to hang about. But she had never dreamed it would happen so quickly. In the event, neither of them had time to make plans about parenthood. Judy miscarried when she was just seven weeks pregnant. The couple were devastated but determined to try again. Within a few months Judy was pregnant again. This time, she was nearly five months pregnant when, for no reason, the baby just died in her womb. 'I felt empty. My breasts were producing milk but the baby was dead.' The days that followed were some of the worst in Judy Finnigan's life. Having been told by doctors that the baby was dead, she was then told she would have to give birth to it.

For Judy, giving birth to her dead baby was a safer option than having a Caesarean section. In cases like hers, where the baby dies for no reason, a Caesarean can sometimes be danger-ous for the mother and could have implications for the next pregnancy. Doctors usually prefer to induce labour to make the mother go through a birth which they believe helps her to come to terms with it.

Dr Julia Mont, one of London's top gynaecologists, says mothers whose babies have died in the womb are often given little hand and foot ink prints of their baby together with a lock of hair. 'Women never get over that kind of death,' says Dr Mont. 'And even if they go on to have two or three more babies, the one they lost is still very much on their minds. These days we make up a book of information about the dead baby to give to the mother. It's a record for her to prove that, yes, she was pregnant, and yes, it was a living event. People on the outside are often too embarrassed to talk to mums who have lost their babies this way. The book is to help her to grieve and remind her that her child was once alive. That it did happen. People tend to treat this kind of situation like it's a miscarriage. It's not, it's a death.'

Judy was desolate at the loss of her son. 'Everyone felt so desperately sorry for her at the time,' says one of the women who worked in the Granada production office. 'To have to carry around a foetus that you know is dead and then to have to give birth to it has got to be one of the worst things that can ever happen to a woman. And Judy was devastated by it. We all kept telling her that she was still young enough and healthy enough to have more children but at that stage she was too upset to listen.'

Says another of Judy's friends at the time: 'It was a very bad time for her. I remember Richard was terribly supportive and everyone in the office sent cards and letters of condolence. We felt for her. It was a monstrous thing for any woman to have to go through.'

It took a long time before Judy was able to talk about the

death of her baby to anyone but finally she spoke about it in *Woman* magazine in 1992, in an effort to help other women who might have experienced the same horror.

'I had gone for a routine scan and the baby, a boy, had just died. It was simply devastating. No one ever really knew why it had happened. The doctors did a post-mortem but they rarely know for sure why these things happen.'

Judy has her own ideas about why her little boy died. She believes it had something to do with the fact that she had a huge cyst on one of her ovaries during the pregnancy. 'I think the cyst swallowed up all the surrounding tissues in my womb and the baby was not able to be sustained.'

The death was a cruel blow to the couple who had so desperately wanted to consummate their love with a child. Richard was crushed. Here was a man who, when he was with his first wife, had always said that he never wanted to be a father. But that was before he met and fell in love with Judy. Then his doubts about fatherhood disappeared overnight and he'd been thrilled when he'd discovered she was pregnant. To lose one baby at seven weeks and then another at five months would have been enough to break up many couples. But even though he was grief-stricken, Richard set aside his own feelings and tried to help his wife.

Judy was inconsolable, not just for the son she had lost but because she knew time was running out. She was hurtling towards 40 and as far as her biological clock was concerned, she was on countdown. She'd desperately wanted to have children with Richard. Now she didn't know whether she would ever be able to give him a child of his own. And, no matter how many times he said it didn't matter, the thought still terrified her.

But three months later all Judy's fears disappeared with the news she was pregnant again. 'It was a wonderful time and it was a terrifying time,' Judy remembers. 'I was terrified Jack was going to die too, so if I didn't feel him kick for half an hour I'd fly into a panic.'

Everything should have been wonderful after Jack was born. He was healthy, he was beautiful, he was everything they'd dreamed of. But Judy had forgotten just how much hard work was involved in having a new baby in the house. She was exhausted all the time. The two miscarriages and her pregnancy had left her mentally and physically drained. Richard had been wonderful. He'd done all the cooking and shopping while Judy tried to gather her strength. But five months after giving birth to Jack, just when they thought they had weathered it all, Judy discovered she was pregnant again. 'I remember waking up to tend to Jack one night and thinking, Oh my God, I can't go through all this again.'

The terror that she might not be able to cope with another new baby haunted Judy throughout her pregnancy. She was nearly 40 years old and she had been pregnant for the last two-and-a-half years. She had wanted babies, but not so many and so soon. However, the clouds of fear and depression that had engulfed her during the nine months of her pregnancy lifted the instant she saw her baby daughter's beautiful face for the first time.

'Having a baby girl after three boys was fabulous. She hardly ever cried and was easily the most placid of all my babies.'

But two miscarriages and two children in rapid succession could not fail to take their toll. After the initial joy of Chloe's birth, Judy found herself in the grip of a deep, black depression that threatened to overwhelm her. Everything seemed hopeless. Nothing, not even her two beautiful babies, her sons or her new husband brought her any joy. Judy didn't know it at the time but she was suffering from a severe case of post-natal depression. 'It was hardly surprising. I'd been pregnant virtually non-stop and my hormones were all over the place. Having babies in your thirties is tiring enough. I was forty when I gave birth to Chloe.'

Judy says that in the six months following her daughter's birth she went completely downhill. 'I knew I'd hit rock bottom because I spent every day crying my eyes out and I just couldn't get out of bed. I was depressed for more than ten months, but I didn't realise what was causing it. I know now it was post-natal depression but I didn't recognise or understand it at the time, which is why I didn't do anything about it. All I knew was that I was at the end of my tether.

Richard and Judy

'Richard was fantastic during that time and it was especially hard for him because he had no idea what the problem was either. Neither of us imagined it was depression because you always imagine that's a disease other people suffer from.'

7 Judy's Fight with the Flab

I T WAS 1990, two years after *This Morning* went on air, and just three years after the traumatic birth of Judy's daughter Chloe. Judy and Richard just needed to relax and get away from it all. They had chosen the idyllic location of Antibes on the French Riviera, one of their favourite places to unwind after a gruelling nine-month run of the show. This was to be their 'special' time together, the two weeks every year they blocked out of their busy calendars just to be alone.

Richard has always insisted on spending time privately with his wife. He *loves* being a husband and father but he *needs* time alone with his wife so they can learn to be lovers again. They relish these little 'honeymoons' because they give them a chance to rediscover and rekindle the passion that flared when they first met.

Passion has always been an integral part of Richard and Judy's relationship. The sexual frisson between them has been obvious and overwhelming from the start. It was what tipped off the staff of the *Granada Reports* newsroom that they were more than 'just good friends'.

That was in the early days when all Judy and Richard had was time and eyes for each other. But marriage, fame and the stress of juggling the responsibilities of a family and two celebrity careers can take a toll on desire.

Richard himself has acknowledged on *This Morning* that there is a strong sexual charge between them and that sex is a very important part of their marriage. He has also admitted that eight hours of live television every week is enough to put a strain on any relationship, however enduring. In an effort to recharge themselves, the couple regularly take time out alone.

They might be mummy and daddy to four children, but they feel they deserve time to be lovers as well.

There seemed no better place to relax together than glorious, sun-kissed Cap d'Antibes. Dazzling white beaches, glittering azure water, the scents of lavender and pine trees, ice-cold cocktails appearing at the wave of a hand . . . it was perfect, exactly what they needed to restore themselves after the latest run of the series.

They arrived from Manchester, Judy looking smart in a polka-dot dress and jacket and Richard casual in jeans and blazer. It didn't take them long to wind down, nor to recapture the romance that had been put on hold for the past few months. Richard and Judy looked blissfully content as, day after glorious day, they lazed on squashy blue and white striped loungers on a beach just 30 yards from the three-star Hôtel du Levant.

'They were just like a couple of honeymooners,' said one of the guests at their hotel. And they were. They hugged and kissed in the blazing sunshine. Richard, as always, was gallantly attentive to his wife. He brought her drinks and rubbed suntan lotion on her back. He was constantly on hand to kiss and stroke and pay attention to the woman he loved.

And then came *those* pictures.

A photographer working for the *Sunday People* sneaked a series of photos of Richard and Judy relaxing on the beach. He snapped them kissing tenderly as they lay side by side on their sunbeds. He caught them lovingly rubbing suntan oil into each other's back. No intimate gesture went unnoticed – and neither did the fact that Judy was no longer a trim size 12, but a more generous size.

Antibes was one of Richard and Judy's favourite holiday destinations, but although they didn't know it then, this was to be their last visit. 'It feels tainted now,' Judy was to say later.

Like most well-known adages, 'The camera never lies' tells only part of the truth. It would be fairer to say that the camera reveals what the photographer *wants* to see – in this case candid shots of an off-duty celebrity looking less than glossily perfect.

In her itsy-bitsy pink bikini it was undeniable that Judy

Finnigan was a big girl. It didn't matter that there were millions of other women on beaches the world over who looked plumper in their bikinis than Judy did. These women weren't being paid handsomely to pop into our living rooms every day. These women weren't the other half of a couple dubbed the king and queen of daytime TV.

They went into overdrive with the shots sneaked by the paparazzo. The pictures of Judy were reprinted again and again. Endless features were spawned on what the 40-something woman should do to look her best on the beach. Professors of metabolics pontificated on the phenomenon of middle-aged women and their 'declining activity levels'. Even the 'Fat is Fabulous' brigade got involved, and asked what was so bad about a fuller-figured mother of four?

It was of course the 'silly season', when even the most trivial of events can be blown up out of all proportion to fuel fruitless speculation and fill those yawning tabloid pages. *Everyone* had an opinion on those revealing pictures which were, after all, taken without their subject's knowledge or consent.

Judy Finnigan was absolutely devastated.

The phone call from Granada about the *Sunday People*'s 'scoop' came through to Richard and Judy's home in Manchester the weekend they got back from Antibes. The company press office and executives from *This Morning* gently tried to prepare Richard and Judy for the storm that was about to break around their heads.

Says a female former reporter, who worked with Judy on *Granada Reports*, 'When I saw those pictures I felt really sorry for Judy. It's so bloody hard for women in the media just to survive, never mind having to cope with that.'

'The press criticisms about her weight hurt her terribly,' says an old friend from Granada. 'You would have to be unbearably arrogant *not* to be hurt by that kind of attack.'

Vanessa Feltz, a one-time presenter on *This Morning*, who left the programme when she landed her own chat show, says: 'Judy gets upset about all the media carping because she never set herself up as a great-looking, slim TV star. She always said she was a busy wife and mother of four.

'She never pretended to be some beautiful catwalk model who's sexy and desirable. I think that's why the digs about her weight hurt so much.'

From the moment Richard and Judy were known to be back home, the press descended in full force. Their phone never stopped ringing. No sooner did they get the number changed than someone would 'leak' it to the press and they would be besieged once more.

Granada didn't feel *too* much damage had been done by the pictures, but still they had to keep a careful eye on the couple to make sure that there was nothing the press could latch on to to make even more capital of the situation. They might have preferred it if their star could have shed a few pounds but there was no way they were going to make an issue of it. Whether it was because she genuinely didn't care about her weight, or because she was unable to do anything about it, Judy had already made it quite clear to TV executives that she was not going to diet simply to stop the baying of the tabloids.

People from the press office were despatched to Richard and Judy's house in Old Broadway, Didsbury, to talk them through the strategy for the next few days. But when they arrived Judy was just on her way out to a children's birthday party with Chloe and Jack – and carrying a huge cake.

It is one of Judy's more surprising traits that despite her years in journalism, and the often extremely intrusive personal scrutiny she has come under, she always expects the best from those around her. It simply hadn't occurred to her that a further furore could easily be manufactured if the press were to photograph her carrying a big gooey birthday cake at this particular moment.

One of the press officers at Granada gently explained to her that this was precisely the photo opportunity the tabloids had been waiting for. She was incredulous but agreed to take his advice. He took the cake from her, waiting till the kids had piled into the back of the family's Volvo and Judy had slipped into the passenger seat at the front. Then he gave her the cake to hold on her lap. The photographers could see they had been well and truly scuppered.

'What they didn't know,' he says, chuckling, 'is that the whole family then headed for MacDonald's where Judy tucked into a king-sized hamburger.'

The incident is most interesting for what it reveals about Judy. Although she knows she is a celebrity, with a face instantly recognised wherever she goes, she has never quite been able to fathom the level of attention that she and her husband attract. Maybe because she has never been a vain woman or the type of presenter who enjoys being publicly fêted, she finds both the press's and public's preoccupation with her private life unnerving and irritating. She genuinely doesn't understand why anyone would be interested in her, beyong watching her on *This Morning*. And she heartily wishes people weren't so obsessed about her figure!

Judy Finnigan is blessed with a beautiful face, but for her this has never been enough. Maybe it was the harsh, frugal years of rationing that made her parents encourage their bonny baby to eat, or maybe she was genetically programmed always to be overweight. Whatever it was, the problem was to cause Judy anguish and insecurity throughout her life. Because, no matter how many times she has said she doesn't care what the press writes, friends who know her well know that she does. They know that the jeers and jibes cut deep – as they would with any woman.

'When she says she doesn't care what people say she is putting on a brave face to the world,' says a friend who has known Judy for more than twenty years.

Ben Frau, Judy's former dresser and a friend, says, 'I was abroad when [the photographs] were published and when I came back Judy never mentioned them. I wouldn't be in the least bit surprised if those pictures hurt her terribly.'

'Judy has never been able to accept that a woman can be overweight and still be attractive,' says one of her lifelong friends, Clarissa Hyman. 'She has had a conflict about her weight for as long as I can remember. She has never really believed that she was attractive even though, rationally, she must have known she was, because there were always men around, telling her how gorgeous she was.'

Judy was never grossly overweight when she was a child. Friends at school remember her as an undeniably pretty child who was a bit 'chunky'. In her teens people dismissed the extra weight as 'puppy fat' and said it would disappear as she grew up. But it didn't. It might have helped if Judy had forced herself into the gym now and then in those days or taken part in the punishing range of field sports offered on Manchester High's curriculum. But she hated games. Right from being a little girl she always preferred the warmth of a cosy classroom or the refuge of her room at home to the great outdoors, with its muddy fields, cross-country runs and sprained ankles. Games might have been the one thing she couldn't do, but the quick-witted little girl's excuses for ducking out of them deserved top marks for ingenuity.

Throughout her teens the weight problem persisted. She was never really fat but she was never able to wear the clothes that her friends managed to squeeze into. Twiggy, with her flat chest and her androgynous body, was all the rage then, but the fashion she generated – the teeny tank tops, the figure-hugging hipsters, the micro mini skirts – was not designed with a buxom teenager in mind.

'She was forever on a diet like the rest of us,' recalls an old schoolfriend. 'We were always eating grapefruit and boiled eggs and dreaming that one day we'd look like Jean Shrimpton.'

The crash diets continued throughout Judy's presenting career at Anglia and Granada. It wasn't that she was particularly vain – she has never spent much time looking at herself in mirrors. As far as Judy is concerned, the only 'mirror' that matters is her man. It is what Richard thinks of her face, her figure, her clothes, that really counts with her.

If on screen Judy can occasionally be subtly assertive, the interviewer who cuts to the heart of the discussion, off screen, in her private relationship with the man she loves, she is more deferential, valuing his opinion above all others.

Her clothes, for instance, must meet with his approval. The form-fitting suits, the short skirts, the sheer 15-denier tights and stiletto heels that have become her trademark on *This Morning*, are all for *him*. Richard finds them sexy and his wife likes to please him. If the wardrobe department produces a suit or an outfit that Richard isn't sure about, Judy will never wear it again. If he tells her she looks good in something, she will wear it constantly.

The fashion and wardrobe girls are given short shrift if they suggest a change of style for Judy – flat shoes instead of stilettos, opaque tights instead of sheer. Her reaction will always be, 'Oh, no. Richard doesn't like them.'

When Richard *does* approve, he is open and unstinting in his praise. There was one morning a couple of years ago when Judy was walking out of her dressing room. She looked particularly good that day and Richard, who was on his way to the studio floor, suddenly stopped dead in his tracks when he caught sight of her. He walked over to where Judy stood chatting and said, 'Darling, you look absolutely wonderful.' And with that he dragged her into a nearby room, saying to the group of open-mouthed people who were watching: 'Would you please excuse us? I just have to kiss my wife.' And closed the door behind them.

'They are totally obsessive about one another,' says an ex-member of the *This Morning* team. And that kind of obsession usually comes from a relationship that has maintained a strong sexual charge.'

Because Richard's opinion is so important to Judy, it can be difficult for the show's dressers and make-up artists to employ the full range of their professional expertise on her. But one man has succeeded triumphantly.

Lee Din was brought to *This Morning* by the programme's first editor, Dianne Nelmes. For years he had run a successful hairdressing business in the Whitefields area of Manchester. Women would travel for miles to secure an appointment with the man reputed to have magic in his fingers. They would even pay for him to go to their homes if they needed to look good for a special occasion.

Lee is a gentle, deeply empathic man. Women enjoy his company because they instinctively feel he understands them and they can trust him.

And so it was with Judy. She immediately felt at ease with

this shy, funny, good-looking Indian man, one of a family of ten brought up in the back streets of Salford. She could confide in him, and talk frankly about those aspects of her appearance that bothered her. And very slowly, very gradually, Lee gave her a totally new look.

'He absolutely transformed her,' says one of the production team. 'It was a real Cinderella job. He very gently took her in hand and did a major make-over job on her. When he had finished she was unrecognisable from the woman who had worked on *Granada Reports*. He made her look absolutely gorgeous.'

But Lee had more luck with Judy's face and hair than the rest of the team had with her TV wardrobe. She at first strongly resisted all efforts to tone down what was seen as an over-the-top *Dynasty*-style look.

Says a former member of the team: 'On television, classic, beautifully designed clothes work best. A very strong look can be achieved with simple, unadorned tailoring. But you couldn't get Judy to understand that. In the beginning she would refuse to wear understated clothes like that. She has this very northern thing that if you "have it" you've got to "flaunt it".

'She didn't like classic clothes. She liked jackets that had piped edges and stripes and bits of things on them. She loved frills and flounces and lots of gold jewellery. That's what used to puzzle other women. They'd see Judy wearing these over-the-top clothes and they could never understand what men saw in her. But Judy knew exactly what the attraction was. She knew that it is the obvious that appeals. It's the same reason that you see her crossing and uncrossing her legs a lot on TV. Her husband tells her she's got the best legs in the world so she shows them off. It might sound bitchy but the thigh crossing does get her noticed.'

Over her eight years at *This Morning*, Judy's style has been subtly reworked and changed by those responsible for her wardrobe. Many of her clothes in Manchester were supplied from the shop Pollyanna in Barnsley. The owner regularly flew to Paris and Milan to pick out clothes she thought would suit her many wealthy and discriminating clients, including other showbiz personalities.

Other outfits are bought for Judy at Harvey Nichols and other top stores in London, and she has a particular fondness for Frank Usher – a widely available label not half as expensive as some of the other designer clothes, such as Jean Muir, picked out by her fashion advisers.

But Judy's favourite clothes period on *This Morning*, the time she felt she was wearing clothes that were absolutely her, was when her wardrobe was being designed by her dresser, Ben Frau.

A small balding man in his late thirties, Frau was renowned for his own cheerfully eye-catching style of dress. When he arrived at *This Morning* to work as a wardrobe assistant, he was already creating one-off designs for actress Maureen Lipman.

Ben's brief at *This Morning* was to create a collection that would please both the star *and* the viewers. Those who knew Judy believed it to be an impossible task, but Ben had a way of dealing with her and instinctively understood the presenter's style. So, after consultations with Judy, he designed a collection of brightly coloured, big-shouldered, 'power suits' that Judy adored. The short skirts and the tight jackets perfectly suited her need to be flamboyant.

Granada was more than happy with the arrangement. Ben Frau's clothes were what Judy wanted and they were a lot cheaper than some of the designer labels they'd been forking out for.

But in later years, as *This Morning*'s budget increased, Granada executives decided that Judy's look had to change again. Ben's bold clothes had been fine for the glam, glitzy late eighties, but in the early nineties they wanted Judy to have a sleeker, more sophisticated look. And that change of style was the subject of a series of high-level meetings between *This Morning* executives, fashion advisers and Judy's own dresser.

These days, before the start of the new season's programmes, the people involved in choosing her new wardrobe meet to watch video tapes of the latest trends in design and are asked to give their views on what would best suit Judy. Clothes are then bought 'on approval' and it is the dressers' job to convince

Judy they will suit her. If she is uncertain, they are sent back to the shop.

Since the early days of *This Morning*, the budget for Judy's clothes has more than quadrupled. In the late eighties it would be rare for the cost of her entire wardrobe for the nine-month run to exceed £5,000. These days that figure would barely cover the cost of three designer suits. The budget allowed for a season nowadays is likely to be around £30,000.

But when Judy arrives at the studio early every morning, it will certainly not be in designer gear. She and Richard were sometimes chauffeur-driven to the Liverpool studio in a company car, but as often as not they drove themselves the 40 miles from their Manchester home to Liverpool. When they stepped out on to the cobbles at the studio door, Judy's face was almost always totally bereft of make-up and she would be wearing old tracksuit bottoms, Reebok trainers and little white socks.

'She looked adorable,' says Lesley Ebbetts, *This Morning*'s former fashion adviser. 'She looked eleven years old when she arrived at the studio in the morning. She had tiny feet and they would be wrapped in these little white socks and shoved into her Reeboks. I always thought she looked good like that.'

It is a depressing fact of showbiz life, however, that if a paparazzo ever photographed Judy in this informal guise there would no doubt be another tabloid inquisition and never mind the fact that she is only doing what she is paid to do – waiting until it is the right time for her to put on her make-up and smart clothes and shine before the camera.

Part of Judy Finnigan's appeal, for her daytime audience at least, is the fact that despite her struggles with her weight, she still looks good enough for them to feel slightly in awe of her. They know that she has four children and a busy life off screen where she shares many of their own problems and concerns. They are realistic enough to accept that nobody can look cool and soignée the whole time, and so they accept *those* photographs for the snatched and sneaky invasion of her privacy they were. Despite the press's sneering and often hurtful comments, Judy's audience still sees her as a more glamorous version of themselves.

Says her friend Ben Frau: 'Judy is the woman who just happens to be on TV then goes home to her kids, has supper, makes them do their homework then puts them to bed. People love her for it.'

8 A Day in the Life of Richard and Judy

VERY FEW PEOPLE ever got famous by just being ordinary. Not, that is, until Richard Madeley and Judy Finnigan exploded on to our screens back in 1988. Never before in the history of programme making had there been a show that made television out of giving step-by-step instructions on how to iron a shirt. And never before had there been two sexy presenters who weren't just man and wife but were so passionate about each other that their on-screen flirting became an integral part of the show's format.

But besides the frisson which sparked between Richard and Judy on screen, there were continual declarations from them that just because they presented hours of live television every week, it didn't mean they were any different from the people watching their show. They insisted they had the same highs, the same lows, the same family problems, the same money worries, as two million fans who tuned in to watch them every day. They were, as they were quick to point out, just an ordinary couple dealing with everyday life, with the same fears and uncertainties as everyone else.

And with their frank, funny, and sometimes embarrasingly honest attitudes to family life, Richard and Judy managed to win over not only cynical TV bosses but, more importantly, convinced everyone at home that here was a *real* couple. These were two genuine, unaffected people broadcasting from the unfashionable north in what looked more like someone's cosy front room than a television studio. And their talent seemed to be as simple as talking *to*, as opposed to *at*, their audience.

This Morning's famous 'cosy' format nearly became even more of a family affair when the show's producers suggested that Dan and Tom, Judy's twin boys, should become part of the show's format – but with a healthy disrespect for stardom, the boys said no. Their school friends would laugh at them!

Richard and Judy created an air of intimacy with the viewers by letting slip little glimpses into their lives in a way that made everyone watching feel part of the Madeley/Finnigan family.

But how much do any of us *really* know about their day-to-day lives? What do they do after the programme? Where do they go? What is it really like to be them? And is it possible that the couple who have been dubbed the king and queen of daytime can still be the couple next door?

Richard and Judy may have started out as an average couple trying to earn a living with a mortgage round their necks and four kids to look after, but what is their life like now? With a joint salary of £1.5 million a year, they can hardly lay claim to money worries any more. But have these been replaced by other problems? Why do the couple who once spoke to almost any newspaper that asked, now jealously guard their privacy virtually to a point where no one is allowed into their lives? Just what is a day in their life like? Would the viewers who imagine they are part of Richard and Judy's lives, ever be able to step into their shoes for a single second?

Until August 1996, when the couple moved to London, they started every day from their rambling old Victorian house in Didsbury, the fashionable Manchester 'village' that in the seventies and eighties became the natural location for trendy media types. Because their 'job' was 40 miles away in Liverpool, Richard and Judy both had to be up at 6am to see to their four children – twins Tom and Dan, from Judy's first marriage, and their own two, Chloe and Jack.

Judy, who is always desperately worrying that she doesn't get enough sleep, finds it harder to get out of bed than her husband. She is fanatical about getting her 'eight hours' every night and tries to be in bed by 10pm. But as a busy mother of four who refuses to have full-time help in the house, and whose job just happens to be talking to two million people on national television every day, she doesn't always manage to get to bed at the time she needs to.

Richard, on the other hand, has boundless energy and seems much more able to cope with the frenetic lifestyle that leaves his wife exhausted. He doesn't need as much sleep as Judy and because of his inherent energy is much quicker and brighter than his wife in the morning. While she likes to slide silently into her day, with as little noise and fuss as possible, he prefers to chat, listen to the radio and joke around with the children.

When in Liverpool, both would shower and dress before waking Tom, Dan, Jack and Chloe. Richard would usually slip on jeans and trainers for the drive to Liverpool, while Judy would throw on leggings and maybe a tracksuit top. Both would wash and towel dry their hair when they got up but neither of them would bother too much about how it looked because the minute they hit the studio it would be taken care of by professionals.

Once dressed, Richard and Judy would head for the kitchen to get breakfast ready for their children, who by this time would be wandering sleepily about upstairs. Tom and Dan are both eighteen now and are capable of looking after themselves. But Jack, who is eleven, and Chloe, nine, both still need to be fed and dressed.

But even as they rush around getting the children ready for school, Richard and Judy would know that sitting on the front doorstep, alongside the milk, is the script for that day's programme. It would have been there all night, dropped off some time the previous evening by a Granada driver under strict instructions that he must never, under any circumstances, disturb the celebrity couple by ringing the doorbell. Richard and Judy have made clear to Granada that when they are at home they do not wish to be disturbed.

'The final scripts are prepared the night before,' says a former producer on the programme. 'In an ideal world they would be ready about 9pm but because things are changing all the time we sometimes don't get them to Richard and Judy's house until after midnight. All the drivers are told that they must never disturb them. Their instructions are just to leave the script on the step and creep back to their car as quietly as they can.

So, as Judy busied herself in the kitchen making tea and toast, Richard would unlock the front door and collect the script and the producer's notes which detail the order and the content of that day's programme.

By the time Richard and Judy were ready to leave the house at around 7.30am, the children's nanny would have already arrived. While being given a few last-minute instructions by Judy, Richard would be loading their briefcases, newspapers, and whatever else they would need for the day into the back of the family's Volvo estate.

In the early days of *This Morning*, Granada used to send a car and a chauffeur to drive the couple the 40 miles into Liverpool. But in recent years, probably prompted by Judy's need for peace and quiet in the mornings, they have preferred to get to the Albert Dock under their own steam. But even though they might have been alone on their journey into work, there was little chance for the couple to relax. This was work-intensive time for them, the first opportunity to go through the notes on that day's programme. The script that has been delivered to them is typed on light blue paper. The colour blue signifies that this is the final draft of a script which started life the previous afternoon on white paper at a programme conference in a room next door to the editor's office and later graduated through four or five more drafts before it was polished into the final product.

While reading through all the paperwork, Richard and Judy would make a conference call from the car to that day's producer to discuss whether or not they like the way the show has been put together.

This working pattern might of course change now that the couple have moved to London. Their smart new home in Hampstead is not far from the LWT studios in Central London so there won't be enough time to do the preparation work they need to do en route. But despite the fact they always had a mountain of work to do before they reached the Albert Dock, Richard and Judy still found time to have the occasional row. Once Judy had read out relevant stories from that day's newspapers to her husband and gone through the various sections of the script with him, she liked to mull over her own notes in total silence. Richard, on the other hand, preferred to have Radio Four's *Today* programme blaring out all the major news stories of the day. He turned it on, and she, in infuriated silence, tried to ignore it.

But their rows were silly rather than serious. Richard and Judy knew there wasn't time to bicker because their real energy needed to be focused on the programme they were about to present.

When they arrived at the Albert Dock at around 8.15am, most of the *This Morning* team would have been hard at it since 7am. The producer and researchers putting the programme together would all be furiously working by the time Richard and Judy arrived.

This is probably the most nerve-racking time of the day for the people who have masterminded that day's show. This is the stage they discover that some of the guests have cancelled at the last minute, that planes have been held up due to bad weather, and that some items, particularly the news-based ones, have fallen down because of overnight developments.

As Richard and Judy arrive and make their way to their dressing rooms, Richard is the one who shouts 'good morning' to everyone. Judy, still quiet and wearing no make-up, just keeps her head down and nods to people if she happens to catch their eye.

'Richard is the more personable one of the two,' says one of the producers on the team. 'When he comes in his hair is all fluffy because he's just washed it and he looks ready for anything. He's very charming and says hello to everyone. Judy says barely anything. She looks grumpy but I think it's to do with the fact that she's an incredibly shy woman. She tends to come in without looking at anyone and just scurries to her dressing room. No one sees either of them again until they are dressed, made up and ready to go into rehearsals.'

Once she goes into make-up Judy knows she has an hour to be 'transformed' into her screen persona. By the time she walks into her dressing room, Lee Din, her own personal hair and make-up artist, is waiting to work his magic.

Judy and Lee have become very close in recent years. There are few people she feels able to confide in on the *This Morning* set, but Lee is one of the privileged few. His calming, supportive presence for that first hour is exactly what Judy needs to set her up for the day. Lee, who is also the hair and make-up genius behind the immensely successful programme *Stars in their Eyes*, was always in great demand by Manchester's wealthy women, who were willing to pay vast sums of money for him to style their hair. But now Judy has become so reliant on him, and so insistent that no one can do hair and make-up like him, Granada have moved him to London to be with her at the new LWT studios on the South Bank.

So just after 8.15am Judy settles back in her comfy leather chair and lets Lee get to work. Most days he applies a light, natural-looking foundation to her face and highlights her eyes with flattering neutral colours which look just right for the daytime. Her favourite lipsticks are light, coral-coloured shades.

After Judy's face is finished, Lee sets to work on her baby-fine blonde hair. He will have prepared the style by wetting it slightly and blow-drying it before starting her make-up. But once that's finished it only takes him a few minutes to 'dress out' the hair – which involves Judy bowing her head until it is virtually upside down, and Lee using his hands and the hairdryer to give it added volume. He then sprays a gentle mist of fine lacquer to keep the style in place. Then it's time for Judy's dresser to step in and help her get into what she is wearing that day.

In the hour that Judy is being made up and dressed, the show's producers are loath to disturb her 'But sometimes we absolutely have to,' says one. 'She doesn't like it because for her that time is extremely private.'

By 9.15 Richard and Judy have emerged from their dressing rooms. In Liverpool they were driven the few yards to the studio for the 9.25 'promo'. This is the time they both go on air for the first time to 'trail' that day's programme and give viewers a few tantalising hints of what is to come. Lee, armed with a toolbox overflowing with powders and lipsticks, always travels with them so he can touch up their make-up, which soon begins to shine under the hot studio lights.

Most days Richard and Judy cut the studio journey so fine they make it with only seconds to spare before going on air. 'They do it every single day,' says one of the producers. 'And there are some days Judy doesn't make it at all if she's been held up in make-up. Those are the days when you will see Richard trailing the show on his own and cheerily telling viewers that Judy will be along later. That, of course, is when he is at his best because when it's absolute chaos behind the scenes, Richard keeps cool.'

Straight after the first promo is broadcast, Richard and Judy record another one which is aired at 9.53. Then it's down to the work of reorganising and rewording great chunks of the script. This can be a tense time for everyone in the studio. Richard and Judy are so in tune with *This Morning* that they instinctively know what works and what doesn't. So sometimes, if they see an item which they think is unworkable, they will have no hesitation in changing it. They will even demand that some items be dropped altogether because they don't fit the programme's ethos.

'They are very much in control,' says one researcher who used to work for *This Morning*. 'They have absolute authority and can overrule anything anyone says. If they don't like an item it will be dropped. But having said that, they are terribly professional. They can sense a problem almost before it happens.'

Says a former producer with the programme, 'they will almost always rewrite the script, which is something they have every right to do. But because we have so little time, this is where we get into a bit of bickering and bantering with the rest of the team. But the truth is that they are both good writers and know what works for *This Morning*. They know their stuff and their style and none of us can tell them anything they don't know already. They feel it's their show, they are the editors, and they want to stamp their mark on it.'

But even though the stars of the show can sometimes be temperamental, it is still universally acknowledged that they are the very best at what they do.

'There is enormous respect for how good they are,' says a member of the team. 'They might make life difficult sometimes, but the truth is that when they demand changes in the script, more often than not they are right. And even though all the people who stand in for them when they are away or on holiday are very good, not one of them is a patch on Richard and Judy.'

As 'on air' time edges closer, the adrenaline starts to flow and Richard and Judy get progressively more nervous. Judy continually gnaws at her nails as she races through her script, making last-minute changes. Richard gets jumpy and his face become increasingly serious as he shouts queries across the studio to the floor manager and the cameramen.

Suddenly it is countdown to the opening titles. The couple both make adjustments to their hair and clothing, they sit up straight, and as the floor manager counts them down to 'on air', the tension that just seconds before has been etched across their faces miraculously melts into great big smiles and they launch into live television.

'It doesn't matter how many times you do a live TV show, the adrenaline is always rushing,' says one of the team. 'That's half the fun of it. It's why people in live television do what they do – for the rush.'

While the programme is unfolding on air it is fascinating to watch how Richard and Judy react to the various items they have to present. Most of the people watching at home would expect it to be Judy who would be keen to pick up handy hints from the show's regular cook, Susan Brookes. Not so. It is Richard who races across the studio floor, eager to try out the dish of the day. It is Richard who asks questions about how the dish is prepared, which is probably a clue as to who does most of the cooking at home.

But while Richard can't keep his fingers out of the cooking pots, Judy always looks less interested and anxious to move on to the next item.

Another of the show's regular slots are the medical phone-ins. Here again people might expect it would be the female of the partnership who would be riveted by gynaecological matters. But again it's Richard who pitches in with the personal questions. Occasionally, much to his wife's dismay, he manages to reveal intimate snippets about their own sex life, Judy's pregnancies, and those little physiological problems she often and angrily tells him she'd rather keep private.

For Judy the most challenging part of the show is when she has to do in-depth interviews with members of the public. This is where she excels. By being warm and understanding, often holding hands and reassuringly touching the people she is talking to, Judy manages to delicately extract information in situations that would fox even the cleverest newspaper reporter. In interviews where intelligence and sensitivity is required, Judy is the best. She is also frequently moved by the people she is talking to. They see her emotion and feel more able to confide in her.

It is widely acknowledged that it is she who is the anchor of the programme. Richard is the fun, light-hearted element, but sometimes he has a tendency to veer off course, saying odd things and making daffy comments. It is always Judy who brings things back into line.

One of the most popular sections of the programme is the 'coffee time' slot. In Liverpool celebrity guests were interviewed by Richard and Judy in either the studio or the much grander location of Doyle's, a lavishly decorated area of the Granada building adjacent to the hospitality room.

Doyle's is furnished with deep plush sofas and decorated in rich regency blues. But because conducting an interview in Doyle's meant that Richard and Judy had to leave the studio and dash up flights of stairs into the building next door, the guests had to be pretty special before the presenters would agree to do it.

'It was hilarious,' says one producer. 'Being interviewed in Doyle's was a privilege conferred on people who hadn't the vaguest notion that they were having a privilege conferred on them. We always had this debate when we fixed up a guest: "Is this one with Doyle's or not?" If we thought he or she wouldn't be deemed an A-grade guest by Richard and Judy, we'd say, "Nah, put them on the set."

'The crew would have liked us to send all the guests up to Doyle's because it would have given them a chance to reposition the cameras on set. But Richard and Judy hated doing it unless it was for someone they considered to be worthy.

'The kind of people who were deemed to be good enough for Doyle's were Cliff Richard, Lenny Henry, Mavis and Derek from *Coronation Street* and actor Robert Powell.

But according to the team, Richard and Judy can be as star struck as the viewers when they have someone *really* famous on the show.

Says one of the team: 'They can be really captivated by people. Cliff Richard was a good example. They were both really taken by him.'

Says an ex-researcher: 'I remember the time ex-*Brookside* star, Anna Friel, who played a controversial lesbian character in the series, was coming on the programme. We were all really excited to have got her but Richard and Judy, who didn't watch *Brookside*, had never heard of her. We knew they didn't really want her on the show. But once they had met her and spoken to her for a few minutes, they were completely bowled over.

'All through the interview Anna was pretty and charming and funny and she got on really well with Richard and Judy. Consequently, by the end of it they absolutely loved her and even invited her back.'

Says a producer: 'Both of them love having the really big stars on the show. And so do the team. We know that if we get a really good booking it gives everyone a lift and the whole show goes well.'

When the closing titles roll at around 12.15pm every day, Richard and Judy step outside the studio where there will always be a handful of fans waiting to catch a glimpse of Britain's most famous married couple. Richard and Judy always wave or pause to say a brief hello, and then in Liverpool it would be straight into the waiting car which whisked them the 500 yards to the newsroom and straight into a production meeting where the programme editor, the producer and various researchers would be waiting to do a post-mortem on the programme.

If it has been a particularly good show everyone will study it to try and understand why. If it has gone badly there will be heated discussions as to why and how this can be prevented in the future.

Even if these meetings are sometimes a little turbulent, ruffled feathers are soon smoothed by the chilled bottles of white wine brought out of the editor's fridge the minute Richard and Judy appear. There are also calorie-laden sandwiches and tasty morsels of seafood laid out around the room so that the top-ranking members of the team can snack while they talk.

For Richard and Judy this is probably the first time they will have eaten that day, and this kind of snacking may have exacerbated Judy's weight problem. Because of her hectic schedule there is never time for three balanced meals a day. She never eats a proper breakfast. Lunch is likely to be snacks in the office or on the odd occasion she and Richard would stroll to a local restaurant on Albert Dock. When she gets home she snacks and nibbles while she is making tea for the kids. The only proper meal she and Richard have is when the kids have gone to bed in the evening. These are often ready-prepared meals that have been taken straight from the freezer and popped into the microwave.

Says slimming expert and friend of Judy's, Sally Ann Voak, '*This Morning* is a very demanding show and to combat the pressure Judy sometimes eats things for comfort that she shouldn't. She never gets the chance to eat balanced meals.'

But tell that to Oprah Winfrey who, as chat show host and owner of her own multi-million pound production company, *still* lost five stone. Maybe the truth is that Judy's time at home with Richard is so limited and special that she doesn't want to spend it eating fat-free food and drinking carbonated water.

But even if she is trying to diet Judy hates to miss her favourite meal of the week – Sunday lunch. When she and Richard aren't working they take it in turns to cook a joint with all the trimmings. Judy's speciality is treacle tart which Richard says could make a grown man weep. The irony is that Richard, at over six feet and eleven and a half stones, can eat like a horse but never puts on an ounce.

When the show first started Richard and Judy used to leave Granada at about three in the afternoon. During the last series, they tended to be gone by around 1.30pm and home for 2.30pm, which meant they could have some private time to themselves before the children arrived home from school.

But even then there is little time to rest. Richard and Judy get straight out of their work clothes, Judy scrubs off her make-up, the nanny goes home, and two of the most famous parents in Britain get down to cooking tea for their kids. A few years ago Judy's mum, who lived just a couple of miles away in Birchfields Road, used to be a constant visitor because she looked after the children when the couple were away working in Liverpool. Today Anne Finnigan is in her eighties and failing eyesight means she can't leave her home without help.

Richard and Judy take their responsibilities as parents very seriously, although Judy still feels enormous guilt about not being able to give her children the kind of time she'd like to. She is always telling people she wishes she were a better mother, and Richard says he too sometimes feels guilty and wishes he was less irritable and much less strict with the children.

But they know that for now they have to do the best they can for their kids in the time they have available to them. So when they get home in the afternoon, the two of them will spend time talking to Jack and Chloe about what's been happening at school and will try to help out with the homework.

For the past few years, sons Tom and Dan have been old enough to go out with friends in the evening, but Jack and Chloe stay snuggled up with their parents in front of the TV until it's time for bed. It is once the children are asleep that Richard and Judy try to dispel the day's tensions with a few glasses of wine. Since they became well known both of them prefer not to go out to restaurants in the evening because of the attention it might create, though occasionally, when they were still in Didsbury, they might have supper with the local builder and his wife who lived just a couple of doors away from them. And sometimes they would go out with Granada executives for a meal. Mostly they preferred to stay at home.

Perhaps that will change now that they are living in London. Both of them used to say that they loved the occasions when they went down to the big city and ate out at the top restaurants. But they knew the reason they liked it so much was because they didn't do it very often and so it was still a big treat. They told colleagues that if they did it all the time it would become boring.

Richard and Judy have no real friends in London and with their manic work schedule it's unlikely they'll have the time to make any, so their lives are still likely to revolve around their home. They choose to wind down by listening to music, watching TV or reading. Both are avid readers and can sit for hours lost in their books. They have learned to give each other space so that neither of them feels the other is crowding in.

At weekends, if they are not working, they will sometimes take the kids out for the day and stop off for a pub lunch. And when they feel up to coping with the stares, they will take Jake and Chloe to the theme parks that they love. But whatever they do, there is rarely any friction between them. Most people who spend virtually every waking hour together could be forgiven for getting tetchy with each other now and then. But such conflict doesn't seem to be a feature of Richard and Judy's relationship. They genuinely seem to get on well.

Judy, of course, has to watch her health because of past gynaecological problems and the tension headaches she is prone to, but generally her health is good. The joke between her and Richard is that no matter how many health problems she has, no matter how much older she is than him, she will still outlive him.

Richard's biggest worry is his heart. His father died when he was just 49, and Richard has always been acutely aware that with the stress of working in TV, the same could happen to him. Because of this fear he has regular heart and cholesterol checks and takes half an aspirin every evening before he goes to bed, which doctors have told him has anti-coagulant properties and will lessen his chances of a heart attack. He also takes a fish oil capsule every day, and his biggest health achievement is that he managed to stop smoking a few years ago, having been hooked for more than twenty years. His father had been a heavy smoker of untipped cigarettes and Richard knew that if he were to cut down his odds of a heart attack, the cigarettes would have to go.

Sometimes, at the end of the day, Richard and Judy fantasise about what they might have done had they not ended up on national TV. There was a time when Judy quite fancied being a doctor and others when she wanted to be a writer. Both talk about leaving the rat race and going to live in a big house in the country. But for now at least, they know that's not possible. They have just started a brand new chapter in their career, and while there are times when Judy might feel she's ready to throw in the towel, Richard still feels he has mountains to climb.

The reality is that for the next two years at least, it will be bed by 10pm in readiness to jump back on the treadmill that is *This Morning*.

9 The Pressures of Fame

LORD BYRON ONCE SAID, 'I awoke one morning and found myself famous.' And so it was with Richard Madeley and Judy Finnigan when, thanks to *This Morning*, they were suddenly catapulted from regional obscurity and an uncertain future into the dizzy, star-studded heights of fame.

It was the kind of fame Richard Madeley had always dreamed about when he was a young reporter at Border Television. For him, being recognised was proof that you had 'made it', or were at least on your way. Fame has remained important to him because he knows that, in television, it is inextricably linked to success. But for his wife there have been times when it has proved a double-edged sword.

Even when she was a regional presenter on *Granada Reports*, Judy was never totally at ease in the public eye – which was strange when, for most people in television, one of the attractions of the job is its high-visibility factor. While her fellow presenters used to revel in the whispers of recognition, or perks like getting the best tables in restaurants, Judy hated it. She didn't want people eyeing her up while she was out shopping. She didn't want people staring at her while she was having a drink with friends. To her it was, and still is, an intrusion. While her husband accepts and enjoys the fact that fame goes with the territory and the £1.5 million pay cheque, it is something Judy still finds hard to acknowledge.

Until 1996 she had turned down press interviews for the previous four years. She even refused a rumoured £20,000 fee for allowing *Hello!* magazine to do a photo spread in a country house hotel, despite the fact that Richard and Granada executives were keen to do it. It was Judy who put her foot down one morning in the editor's office and said she would not share any more of her private life than she already had.

The problem lies in Judy's reluctance to accept that her rôle as queen of daytime means she can never fully realise the privacy she naturally craves. She has convinced herself that she and Richard are 'ordinary' people and can't see why anyone should be interested in their private lives. She gets very defensive when people comment on the way she and Richard are happily married and also work together.

'I feel I must apologise for being married. The critics seem to hate the fact that we work well together. We're far from being the perfect couple but any disagreements or rows we have are wiped out by the adrenaline of being on air. It's very therapeutic for the marriage. By the end of the show we have forgotten about it and are kissing each other again.'

Close friends say Judy is genuinely loving and protective of her children. For her, there is nothing beyond them and her husband – nothing that matters.

She wants to work, and prides herself on doing a thorough and professional job, but frequently feels guilty about the time she is forced to spend away from the children. 'We didn't have children in order to ignore them,' Judy has said.

On set she can sometimes be demanding – but only because she wants the best for her guests and the programme. She hates second-rate work and expects other people to work just as hard as she does. It is no secret, however, that for her the happiest times of the week are those she spends at home with her children.

In the beginning, in the days when Granada's bosses had no idea if *This Morning* would be a success, their two 'star' presenters shared the same facilities as the rest of the programme's crew – or rather, their lack of facilities.

For the first three years the programme was on air there wasn't even a loo in the studio, let alone a private one for Richard and Judy, as there is now – which meant that if either of them needed to pay a visit during the programme they would have to wait until there was a commercial break and then rush out to the public toilet on the dock. On numerous occasions Richard and Judy were to be seen, standing in their respective queues, with mike pack and talkback still attached. Despite the fact that they were doing a high-pressure job, timed to the last second, neither of them would ever try to jump the queue but would stand patiently waiting their turn, praying they'd make it back into the studio in time.

Although the show's success brought them recognition and rewards, Richard and Judy's unassuming personal lifestyle changed little. Until the move to London they lived in Didsbury, a suburb of Manchester – not for them the Cheshire stock-broker belt or the grand stone piles of the Derbyshire Peaks.

There is a part of Judy that is a 'home body' still; someone who values the privacy and comfort of her own surroundings, put together with love and care over the years. The four-bedroomed house in Didsbury was known to be cosy and unostentatious. The kitchen was furnished in pine, and they ate around a family-sized table with a scrubbed top.

In the sitting room were green Draylon-covered sofas and a carpet which bore all the marks of kids having run riot over it. There were toys in the hall, anoraks over the banisters. It was a typical family home, in fact.

When Maggie Colvin was on the programme, giving tips for the stylish redecoration of viewers' homes, Judy would often say wistfully, 'Oh, I wish we could have something like that.' There was of course absolutely no reason why she should not be living in interior-designed luxury – except that it just wasn't her style.

Similarly she is not interested in status symbol cars – she and Richard have an old Volvo estate. She once described cars on air as 'tin cans that get you from A to B'. She can't understand why the more money people earn, the flashier their car gets. She says that if she had her way, their car would be left to rot in the garage.

Because Judy grew up in a background where there was little money to spare, she is extremely careful with it now. She saves for a rainy day because she is realistic enough to appreciate that money and fame don't necessarily last for ever.

She doesn't need to spend money on clothes, as her 'public' wardrobe at least is bought by *This Morning*, so to date her biggest extravagances have been the five trips which she and Richard took to see *Phantom of the Opera* when it was on in Manchester and the family's annual trip to the States.

So far this all adds up to a picture of a remarkably well-adjusted, down-to-earth woman, one who has kept faith with her background and the things that really matter in life, as well as achieving success in the cut and thrust of the television world.

But inevitably there have been sacrifices to be made along the way. Judy and Richard spend nine months of every year working with a speed and intensity which few broadcasters are ever called upon to match. When they are not working they are doing their best to ensure that their children receive the love and attention due to them. This leaves them very short of time and, in Judy's case, energy.

When she first started on *This Morning* Judy was quoted as saying, 'The job itself is fine but then I come home to all the domestic things. When we started I felt overwhelmed by it all. I thought everyone was coping a great deal better than me. Our children deserve a great deal of our time and that is proving harder than I'd anticipated.'

Though she and Richard make it plain in their many on-screen comments and unmistakable body language how very much attuned to each other they still are, Judy says the stresses of everyday life have put paid to much of the romance in their life, hence the all-important little 'honeymoons'. 'By the end of the day I have had it,' she says, 'and crash out in bed around nine-thirty. Our social life has gone completely too.'

A fact that is sadly confirmed by one of Judy's oldest friends. 'She has been caught up in this incredible whirlwind of fame. Maybe when you experience the sort of fame she has, it has to affect you in some way.'

In Judy's case, there seems to be a feeling that she has put behind her several long-standing and once close friendships.

'Part of the problem is that she's not even sure *why* people want to be her friend any more,' says one of them. 'She suspects their motives and believes they only want to know her because of who she is.' Maybe her caution is understandable bearing in mind her high profile.

A couple of years ago Judy ignored an invitation to an old girls' reunion at Manchester High. Says one of the women who went to it: 'We were all really sorry she didn't come. Maybe she thought we would have been scrutinising her all the time. It's a pity she can't see that we don't all have an ulterior motive.

But it is surely significant that few of her friends from the old days, have ever spoken out adversely about her, even though she has upset some of these friends by not staying in touch. One of them says this is a measure of the kind of loyalty she used to inspire.

Judy's distancing of herself is most probably not a matter of simple neglect. It is far more likely that, by the time she has met the demands of job and family, any time she has left is extremely precious to her. Living under constant pressure as she does, is it any wonder that she needs time and space to herself sometimes? She probably misses her old friends as much as they miss her, but that is one of the many sacrifices that fame exacts.

There is an undeniably soft-hearted and kind side to Judy's nature, despite the protective shell she has been forced to grow. Often, after a particularly moving interview on screen involving a disturbing or tragic story, Judy will pull her husband to one side and ask him to write a cheque to boost a fund or a children's charity. She is frequently moved by the plight of other people, as is Richard.

Says a *This Morning* insider: 'They can be really sweet. Sometimes if a guest has had a bad experience, or especially if a sick child is involved, they have written out cheques on the spot to help them. They do have a very caring side which people don't necessarily know about, particularly if it is anything to do with children.'

There are many other instances where Judy's generosity and sweetness of character have made themselves apparent, though people who have experienced this for themselves often talk of how hard it is to pierce the barrier of her reserve initially.

One female reporter who worked with Judy on *Granada Reports* says that while she may have been a wonderful communicator on air, she was not always so in real life. That led some colleagues to think she was stand-offish. The reporter worked with Judy for years but barely had a conversation with her until 'I went to a wedding and she purposely sought me out to talk to me. We talked and talked and were the greatest of friends throughout the party. She was really sweet and loving and interested in everything I said, and I felt like the sun was shining on me. That's the effect she can have on people.'

Says a member of *This Morning*'s production team: 'There is always a barrier with her, but once you get past that she can be warm and friendly and very approachable. I think she feels she can be like that when she's off duty. She does let the guard down when she is not at work. She can also be very kind. I remember once there was someone who worked on the production team whose son was very ill and when she heard about it she made a point of going up to him every day and asking how he was. She was willing to sit there and talk to him about it.'

Jane Green, a former press officer who worked on *This Morning* for a year and a half, says, 'In all the time I worked there I never felt I really knew them. But one night there was a fireworks party and it was the first time I'd seen Richard and Judy off duty. Judy was absolutely lovely and made a point of talking to everyone who worked on the show. It completely changed my opinion of them.'

What has to be remembered is that Richard and Judy, however affable and ordinary they may appear on screen, must each day shoulder an enormous burden. The success or failure of *This Morning* rests largely with them and they are acutely aware of this responsibility.

Vanessa Feltz, who worked on the show for a year and a half, says: 'I got on with them very well though I never really got to know them. They make it a point to keep their distance. I always saw that they were cordial to guests, though never got too close. And now that I have my own show, I understand why that is. You are just so extremely busy that you never get the chance to really talk to them. It's not that you don't like

them or that you look down on them. You just don't have the
time to spend with them.

'As for their relationship with each other, I can tell you that
the whole time that I was there I never once saw them lose their
temper with each other, click their teeth, snap, swear or roll
their eyes at each other. And, believe me, I looked.'

If Richard and Judy do have rows after the programme, they
do it behind closed doors in their dressing room, never in front
of anyone on the studio floor. They might have a discussion
after the programme, but it's never heated when they are
talking to each other.

No one who knows them would argue that, as presenters,
Richard and Judy are the ultimate professionals – brilliant
performers, cool in a crisis, a couple whose on-screen chemistry
can dazzle viewers. Professionally, they are frequently exacting
of their colleagues.

'We used to dread it during the show when Richard and Judy
were interviewing someone and they asked a question and the
interviewee would say something like, "No, that's not quite
how it was. It was like this . . ." ' says one young producer who
has worked on *This Morning*. 'It meant that whoever was
responsible for the item was in for a terrible ticking off. The
way they see it is that if you're not up to the job then you
shouldn't be there. They are the ones who have to front the
show, and if anything goes wrong they are the ones who look
like idiots. You can understand the pressure they're under.'

In many ways Richard and Judy's problems are identical to
those of any manager: the isolation and demands of a top job
make it difficult to sustain friendly, untroubled relations with
people who must report to them and who must, in the way of any
working relationship, occasionally be rebuked or called to order.

Mike Hollingsworth, successful independent producer and
husband of TV presenter Anne Diamond, says, 'It is a pres-
enter-led show, and having worked on a similar show, I know
that you ignore the presenters' feelings about what you should
be doing at your peril.'

And ratings expert William Phillips points out, 'If only
people knew and understood the journalistic skills that go into

making that programme the success it is. It takes great talent to be able to switch from a serious subject to a silly one and then back again. Richard and Judy do that fantastically well.'

Even those who may have been at the sharp end of Richard and Judy's demands can appreciate the pressure that gives rise to them. A former member of the *This Morning* team comments: 'They are total perfectionists. But, at the end of the day, there's a good reason for it. There is so much pressure on a live show.'

And Richard and Judy are more than just the presenters of *This Morning*. They play a large part in 'editing' the show's contents, reviewing the list of proposed items a day in advance and frequently making suggestions of their own for topics they feel should be aired. With years of journalistic experience at their fingertips, they will rewrite scripts if and when they feel it is necessary. But if they are sometimes at odds with producers and researchers on the show, their relations with *This Morning*'s technical crew are said to be excellent.

Very few people are permitted a behind-the-scenes glimpse of Richard and Judy's private lives. An exception is Ben Frau, one of Judy's closest friends, who recalls how she insisted he go to their house for Christmas a couple of years ago.

'They are terribly, terribly private people but we were all having lunch in the studio one day and people were talking about what they were doing for Christmas. I happened to mention I was spending it on my own and Judy screamed, "Oh no you're not!" She and Richard just insisted I spent it with them.

'It was a wonderful Christmas. We ate, drank and watched TV, just like millions of other families. On Christmas Eve Judy cooked up a fantastic roast beef dinner with all the trimmings. We were up until 5am. Richard was playing the guitar and Judy and I were having a good old sing-song. We even had a dance in the living room. It was a crazy night.

'The next day the kids got up and opened all their presents and then we all went out for lunch at a restaurant in Manchester. Afterwards we came back, plonked ourselves in front of the TV and watched *White Christmas* which I'd never seen before.

'It was lovely to be asked. It made my Christmas.'

But the stress of combining a high-pressure public role with that of family life does occasionally tell on Judy. In January 1992 she was sent to a health farm by Granada bosses, suffering from exhaustion brought on by the strain of hosting the show. They also agreed to give her another month's holiday a year, on top of the eight weeks she already had, because it was apparent she was finding the workload a strain.

At the time of her visit to the health farm, she said: 'By the end of the day I've had it. Sometimes I feel I want to climb into a big hole and hide.'

At the beginning of their relationship the age gap between Richard and Judy was barely obvious. Both looked like attractive, upwardly mobile thirty-somethings. Today it's a slightly different story. While stress and their punishing work schedule has done the seemingly impossible and made Richard look more boyish and energised than ever, the effect of the passing years is perhaps more evident in Judy. Eight years of getting up at 6am to do more than 200 hours of live television every year have left her worn out. In a recent interview with the *Telegraph* she said that, although she is eight years older than Richard, it hadn't bothered her at all in the beginning. But she admitted that was changing as she grew older.

'It gets me down a bit more now that I'm forty-eight than it might have done when I was forty,' she said. 'But I think it's more of a problem for other people than for us.'

Colleagues at *This Morning* believe such statements are largely self-defence mechanisms. Many believe that, if it wasn't for Richard, she would give up television.

'That show is relentless,' says an old friend of Judy's. 'I worked on *This Morning* so I should know. Being on it day after day is like being a guinea pig in a treadmill. The work itself isn't hard but it's the relentlessness of it. We used to call it the "women's magazine syndrome". I don't know how Judy can keep doing the same thing over and over. Sure, the programme works, but it has been churning out the same type of stuff now for one hell of a long time.'

Lesley Ebbetts, a former fashion editor on the show, says:

'When I was there we used to have discussions about how unyielding the programme was. There was a time in 1993 when I had to be admitted to hospital for a small women's operation. I was back at work after just a few days but I was feeling the strain. I remember talking about it to Judy one morning and discovering she'd been in hospital a few months before for the same thing. She had come back to work without anyone even knowing.'

Even Judy herself admitted recently: 'I'm so sick of doing the same run to work every morning. Some days I feel I've never left the studio. It's why Richard and I had to make the move to London, otherwise we'd have gone mad.'

But if Judy says the passing of the years has had no effect on her relationship with her husband, she concedes that the age gap, and the fact that she will be 50 in two years' time, could become a professional issue.

'There are some days when Judy looks every one of her years,' says a member of the production team. 'The impression we get sometimes is that on a bad day she would rather retire to the country, grow her hair long and live with her man, her children, and a load of cats and dogs.

'There was an amazing man on the programme last year, an American called Jerry Spence, and he was talking about how you can change your life by destressing yourself. Judy was absolutely captivated by the man and what he had to say.'

Maybe for Judy, after the London move, the next will be to that house in the country and the more relaxed lifestyle she craves and has. Richard, however, seems to thrive on the adrenaline-charged atmosphere of television and seems far less affected by the stresses and strains of their lifestyle. he enjoys the fame and success he worked long and hard to achieve and there is little doubt that he intends to be around for many years to come.

10 Time of Trial

THE DOOR OF CELL NUMBER TWO slammed shut and as the sound echoed around the walls of the stark, unfriendly room, Richard Madeley, TV star and suspected thief, lowered his trembling body on to a chair and wondered how the hell he'd wound up there.

Outside, in the corridors of Fallowfields police station, there was loud bantering and laughter. Richard waited alone in his cell, staring down at his shaking hands. It wasn't enough that the police had stripped him of his dignity, arresting him in the store like that and bundling him into the back of a police van. They had also stripped him of virtually all his possessions: his beautiful gold watch, his wallet, his house keys. They'd even taken the laces out of his trainers. What did they think he was going to do – hang himself with them?

Outside the police station the boys of the national press were growing restless. They'd been waiting nearly five hours for a glimpse of Richard Madeley – and still nothing. He'd been arrested on a charge of shoplifting at Tesco's Didsbury store earlier that afternoon, and although the police wouldn't confirm anything, the reporters and photographers knew they were on to something big. In their late city edition, the *Manchester Evening News* had scooped them all with a picture of the TV star being escorted into the back of a waiting police van. It didn't matter that the photo had been taken by some quick-thinking member of Tesco's staff, on the look-out to make a few quid – they would still have to answer to their editors for it later. But for now they had to concentrate on getting him when he came out. If they missed him this time there really *would* be trouble.

There was a definite buzz about this story. How did a bloke like Richard Madeley come to be arrested for shoplifting? It just didn't seem possible. But then the boys from the nationals had been around long enough to know that anything was possible if you waited long enough. Whether he'd done it or not, this was a story that was going to run and run.

Back at their cosy Edwardian home in Old Broadway, Didsbury, Judy Finnigan had waited anxiously for her husband to return. He'd gone out at lunchtime to get the weekly groceries and by mid-afternoon still hadn't come back. Richard had started doing the family shopping after Judy had had her second miscarriage, and again after Jack and Chloe were born. It was a pattern that had been established when Judy had needed lots of rest and it had remained their habit. She would stay at home with the kids while he did their weekly shop at the Tesco superstore in East Didsbury, just a couple of miles away. But where was he? He'd been gone ages. Judy prayed he hadn't had an accident.

What she didn't know was that, back in Tesco's, Richard was being questioned by Raymond Barlow, the store's general manager, and Angela Orme, the blonde-haired security officer, who had followed him as he left the store and walked to the supermarket's car park. She later alleged before a jury at Manchester Crown Court that she had watched Richard leave the store with his loaded trolley without paying for two bottles of champagne, a bottle of gin and five bottles of wine which were in the compartment at the front. She claimed she had watched him as he unloaded the contents of his overflowing trolley on to the conveyor belt at the check-out, bending over the front compartment several times as he did so. The bottles had been virtually under his nose, she alleged, yet still the TV presenter had made no attempt to take them out and pay for them. The whole event had also been filmed by the store's security camera.

When Angela Orme had confronted the TV star, dressed casually but immaculately in faded blue jeans and a short-sleeved white shirt, he was perfectly genial and simply said he had forgotten to pay for the goods and would do so there and then. She asked him to go back with her to the manager's office, where the police were called.

Half an hour later two uniformed police officers knocked on the door of Raymond Barlow's office where Richard Madeley was still calmly protesting his innocence. After being questioned by the two police officers, the TV presenter was told he was being arrested on a charge of shoplifting and was escorted by the policemen to a waiting police van. Unfortunately for Richard, an employee of the store tipped off the *Manchester Evening News*. That night's front-page picture of the *This Morning* host being walked to the police van sent shock waves through the city – TV's Mr Perfect had been arrested and accused of theft.

At Granada Television, stunned executives were trying to take in the fact that one of their star presenters had been arrested. Liam Hamilton, the editor of *This Morning*, had already rung Ian Haworth in the press office to see what Granada should be doing. Everyone knew Richard had been arrested but no one knew quite how to handle it. By the time Liam picked Ian up outside the Granada offices in Quay Street, Manchester, it was about 8pm. Richard had already been charged and released on police bail. The nationals had managed to get their picture of him as he came out of Platt Lane police station with his solicitor, Michael Green. It had taken the police more than seven hours to question and eventually charge him.

The first offence was alleged to have taken place on 18 August 1990, when he was seen not to have paid for soap powder, champagne and wines and spirits by a cashier, but was not challenged and left the store. The second offence was said to have taken place on 24 August when he was filmed on security video leaving the store without paying for two bottles of champagne, five bottles of wine and a bottle of gin. He was charged by the police initially on the second offence, and with the first 24 hours later.

Back at the house in Old Broadway, Richard fell into his wife's arms. Just a few yards away from Richard and Judy's front door, Liam Hamilton and Ian Haworth waited outside in their car. Neither of them felt they knew quite what to do. They ought to be around in case the couple needed anything, but they didn't want to disturb them at this difficult time. They felt that if they just pitched up on the doorstep, Richard and Judy might be upset, embarrassed or see it as an intrusion. Liam and Ian decided the best thing to do was to ring from the mobile phone in the car. That way they could ask the couple if they needed anything without it being too much of a disturbance.

The next morning the story was all over the papers and the PR wheels at Granada ground into action. Through his solicitor, Michael Green, Richard issued a total denial of the allegations and Granada's bosses insisted categorically that Richard would not be axed from the *This Morning* programme. Moreover, they announced that the launch of the new season's show would go ahead on schedule on 3 September 1990.

And so, just ten days after being arrested and charged with theft, Richard Madeley was back on screen. And if the viewers imagined he was going to try and brush what had happened under the carpet, they were wrong. A decision had been taken at the highest level that the best way to handle what had happened to Richard was to be open and upfront about it. There was no point in trying to hide what had happened or pretend it wasn't serious. It was.

Richard was happy to handle things this way. He had strenuously proclaimed his innocence all along and was 100 per cent convinced he would be acquitted. But still, he knew there would be a lot of pain and embarrassment to go through first. There would also be unbridled media interest. It was best to be open and honest about everything right from the start.

The policy of 'openness' had been decided upon by high-ranking executives at Granada who knew that, with Richard electing to have his case heard at the Crown Court, it could be many months before the case came to trial. Before that there would have to be appearances at the Magistrates' Court, which Richard would have to attend in order to have his bail set and a date for his trial fixed. This in turn could mean there would be days when he wouldn't be able to be in the studio for the start of the show. They knew they couldn't just pretend nothing was happening. The media wouldn't allow them to. More importantly, the viewers would read every detail of Richard's court appearances in the papers. Trying to hide things from them wouldn't just be insulting their intelligence, it would be ratings suicide.

So, in an unprecedented move, it was decided that not only would Richard be allowed to continue hosting the programme with two theft charges hanging over his head, but his court appearances and reactions to them would become part of the show's format.

Being straight with the viewers turned out to have been an inspired move on Granada's part because it conveyed to them that not only did Richard Madeley want to confide in them, but also that his employers believed him to be innocent. It was a brave and controversial stance by a television company.

For most presenters, even the whiff of scandal involving theft would have spelt the end of their TV career, not just because of their employers' reaction, but also that of the viewers. For Richard Madeley it had the opposite effect. Not only did his employers decide to stand by him, but the viewers too came out publicly on his side. As phone calls and letters of support flooded into the studio, Granada realised just how popular their daytime presenter was.

At the time a spokesman said: 'Richard has our full support and faith, along with the strongest hope that his innocence will soon be re-established just as publicly as it is currently being doubted.'

What Granada's active support at the beginning of Richard's ordeal did was to make viewers feel comfortable with what was happening to their favourite TV presenter. The fact that the charges and court appearances were being referred to on air, even joked about, took the sting out of an otherwise very awkward situation. By no longer being treated as taboo, they became almost acceptable. Viewers soon got used to Richard dashing into the studio mid-programme and keeping them up to date with what was happening to him down at the Magistrates' Court, so much so that they didn't want to read about his remand dates and court adjournments in the press – they wanted to hear it straight from the horse's mouth. And Richard obliged.

There was one famous morning when Judy started the show alone, reassuring viewers that although Richard was in court that day he would be joining them later. When he finally did slip into the chair alongside his wife, slightly out of breath as if he had just sprinted from the courtroom, and calmly asked her, 'So how's it going?', she broke off in mid-sentence, looked at her husband tenderly, and said, 'We've missed you.' Richard then proceeded to tell everyone that his case had been adjourned for another two weeks. 'I just thought you'd want to know,' he told viewers.

They loved it. This was a real-life soap opera being enacted before their very eyes. And one that had everything. It had drama. It had pathos. It had love. And, though they didn't know it yet, it had a happy ending.

But even though they had each other and the support of Granada over those difficult months, Richard and Judy didn't receive much support from friends.

Lesley Ebbetts, who was a presenter on the programme at the time, says: 'I rang them at home the day after Richard was arrested because I was absolutely devastated for them. It was difficult to know what to do in those circumstances because you don't want to feel you are prying or interfering. I also thought they would be surrounded by family and friends and that I was probably just going to be an inconvenience.

'Anyway, I decided to ring simply to say, "I'm, here if you need me." I didn't expect them to chat. I just wanted them to know they had my support if they needed it.' Lesley spoke to Judy briefly who then said, 'Hang on, Richard wants to talk to you.'

Richard took the receiver from his wife and proceeded to pour out his heart to Lesley. 'Everything he had been through just fell out,' she says. 'And I realised they had been on their own with this thing for twenty-four hours.' Fame can be a very isolating, lonely business.

As far as the team at *This Morning* could see, Richard was always quite certain that he would be acquitted. If he was worried about the trial, he didn't show it. Whatever fears, whatever stresses he and Judy might be under at home, they never discussed them at work. But Richard knew that people were talking and sniggering behind his back. He'd heard the 'Pinch and Judy' jibes. He suspected there were some people who'd have been glad to see him convicted of a crime he didn't commit. And he was right – there were jealous people all around him.

'I don't think there was ever any real impression of his being guilty,' says a Granada insider. 'To be honest, I don't think it ever occurred to people that he might have stolen that stuff from Tesco. But I think some people might have wanted him to be guilty so that he would get fired.'

It is one of the less attractive human traits that people love to see a fall from grace – as long as it is not their own. And a very public fall from grace, by someone like Richard Madeley, was a spectacle not to be missed.

The trial approached. The date was set for 1 July 1991 in courtroom number five, Manchester Crown Court. There had been many behind-the-scenes meetings at Granada in the weeks leading up to the trial. One of the final get-togethers was a meeting with Dianne Nelmes, by then deputy head of light entertainment, *This Morning*'s editor, Liam Hamilton, Ian Haworth, Granada's head of publicity, and Richard and Judy. The meeting was to talk about the court case and who would be accompanying Judy throughout the four-day trial. Because she was a witness, she would not be able to sit in court to give Richard moral support until she had given evidence. That would mean long lonely hours by herself outside the courtroom and Granada didn't want her to feel isolated. They knew that, with Richard in court, Judy would be the main attraction for the press who would be watching her every move to see how she was bearing up under the strain.

If looks were anything to go by, Judy was actually bearing up very well. She'd lost a lot of weight in the lead-up to the trial, and for the first time in her life it hadn't been difficult. The worry, combined with wanting to look her best for Richard's court appearance, had meant the pounds simply melted away.

Judy was asked by her bosses at Granada if there were any close friends she would like to have with her in court. She said she wanted her wardrobe man, Ben Frau, and hairdresser, Lee Din.

The executives exchanged anxious glances. As far as Judy was concerned, Ben and Lee were the natural choices to take into court. She'd become very close to them in the last twelve months, especially Ben. Even though in the studio the two of them used to bitch and bicker about what clothes Judy was supposed to be wearing, outside they got on like a house on fire. Ben was also very protective of Judy, and when anyone criticised her in front of him he would always defend her, saying, 'Yes, but when she smiles it lights up her whole face.'

He had started working for *This Morning* in September 1990, just ten days after Richard had been charged with theft. Originally he was employed as the wardrobe man, with responsibility for both Richard and Judy's clothes. His friendship with Judy developed over the following months. He seemed to understand her. The two of them had even talked about what would happen to her once the bubble burst and she left *This Morning*.

'Judy wants to write books,' says Ben. 'She has loads of ideas. She just needs time to get them down on paper. The two of us are huge Ruth Rendall fans and we used to swap books all the time. I am convinced that one day she will have a great career as a writer.'

Lee Din was a very different personality, a steadying, calming influence. But still it was felt that neither Lee nor Ben should be by Judy's side at such a difficult time. What would the papers make of her taking her hairdresser and wardrobe man into court with her?

But who was left? Judy had lost touch with most of her friends from the old days. Dianne Nelmes eventually decided it would be best if *she* stayed alongside Judy for the duration of the trial, not just to give her moral support but to protect her from the press. She would also be able to protect Granada's interests. Dianne knew that the publicity surrounding this case was going to be extensive and potentially explosive. It had to

be handled delicately if both the company and the accused were
to come out of it unscathed. It was gently explained to Judy
that though she felt close to Lee and Ben, the press might
misconstrue her taking the man who did her hair and the man
who made her clothes into court. It was the first time in the
eleven months leading up to the tral that she allowed the strain
of what was happening to show and she broke down in tears.

She was beginning to understand that there were people in
the world, cruel people, who would take great delight in
bringing her and Richard down. She could never understand
that kind of malice but knew she had to take heed of it.

On Monday 1 July 1991, the day of the trial finally dawned. It
had taken months of adjournments and remands for this minor
shoplifting case to be brought to court. They had been the
toughest and most stressful months of the Madeleys' entire
marriage, eleven months in which they had been almost torn
apart by the pressure. The couple had never tried to conceal the
facts of the case from their viewers, but they had sought to
conceal their own fears. They had talked about the case on
screen, even laughed about it, never allowing anyone to believe,
even for a moment, that they doubted everything would turn
out OK. 'He always seemed immensely confident he would be
acquitted,' says one member of the *This Morning* team about
Richard's behaviour at this time.

But behind closed doors Richard Madeley was living under
almost unbearable strain. He knew he was innocent but what
would happen if the jury didn't believe him? What would
happen to his job, his family, his future?

He knew it wouldn't be long now before he found out.
Richard also realised that there would always be people who
chose to believe he was guilty even when he was proved
innocent. Just a few weeks before he had been on his way to
the Magistrates' Court for a remand hearing when he came face
to face with the kind of prejudice that was to plague him for
years, even after his innocence was proved.

Richard had been first into the lift at the Magistrates' Court
in Manchester's Crown Square. A couple of other people

followed him and, just as the doors were about to close, three youths pushed their way into the lift. They all stood with their backs to Richard. No one spoke at first and then suddenly the silence was broken by one of them shouting 'Thief!' at the top of his voice. Everyone in the lift went rigid. No one moved. No one spoke. The embarrassment was tangible. But Richard just looked straight ahead. He didn't flinch, didn't speak. Whatever he felt, he kept it to himself. He understood this was how it was going to be.

Richard and Judy both knew that the national press would be out in force on that sunny Monday morning. So they decided to put on a show. Judy had dressed carefully. She'd chosen a pastel suit, matching pale shoes and a white silk camisole. Her blonde bobbed hair had been washed and blow-dried by Lee, and on her ears were a pair of colourful clip-on earrings. Richard was wearing a dark navy suit, a crisp white shirt and spotted silk tie. He was carrying a briefcase.

If either of them was nervous about the day that lay ahead it didn't show as, hand in hand, they strolled across the tree-lined square that led to the concrete steps of Manchester Crown Court. They beamed at the cameras. They even stopped for a few minutes, arms around each other, to pose for pictures. The message was clear: 'We're in this together.'

Inside the courtroom the public gallery was full to bursting. Everyone wanted a ringside seat for this soap opera come to life. They'd started to queue just after 8am on that warm summer's morning just to get a glimpse of TV's golden couple in their most anxious hour. Watching them on TV talking about their lives and problems was one thing. Being there while those problems actually unfolded was quite another.

Just before the case began, Judy leant into the dock to take her husband's hand and whisper some words of reassurance. She wished him good luck, and with her eyes told him she loved him.

Mr Anthony Gee, GC, prosecuting, opened the case. Richard Madeley had pleaded not guilty to two charges of theft. He had been charged with stealing soap powder, wines and spirits from a Tesco store in Manchester on 18 August 1990, and a further quantity of wines and spirits from the same store the following week.

Mr Gee told the jury that Richard Madeley had been captured on film removing bottles of wine and spirits from the supermarket.

'Richard Madeley is a man of good character who is also a television presenter with, no doubt, a substantial income,' he told a hushed courtroom. 'The prosecution allege that, on two separate occasions, Richard Madeley deliberately and dishonestly took a substantial quantity of wines and spirits.' He said that Madeley had been filmed by a supermarket security camera six days after he allegedly took £60 worth of other goods from the same store without paying for them. He said on the occasion he had been caught on camera, the TV presenter had unloaded his shopping on to a conveyor belt and bent over his trolley several times to do so, which, Mr Gee alleged, would have meant the wine and champagne were literally under his nose. But, according to the prosecution, at no time had Mr Madeley made any attempt to take the bottles out of his trolley or bring them to the cashier's attention. 'He paid by cheque a total of £88.92. If he had paid for the whole contents of the trolley the bill would have been £144.34,' said Mr Gee.

He alleged that on the first occasion the TV presenter had been in the store, on 18 August, he had paid £106 for the goods in the body of his trolley, but not for a large bottle of gin, three bottles of champagne, and other drink valued at around £60. The offence was not reported to the police, but on the next occasion Richard Madeley was in the store, which was six days later, a security officer had watched him.

The court heard that store detective Angela Orme had followed Madeley to the car park. She asked him about the bottles and he was alleged to have told her, 'Oh, sorry, I must have forgotten to take them out.'

In a statement to police he was alleged to have said: 'I did not unload the wine because I forgot. I suppose it's like a psychological effect because they are confined in a separate part of the trolley.'

Richard Madeley told police that when he was stopped outside by security staff, he 'immediately realised and admitted his mistake', but was given no opportunity to pay for the items and instead taken straight to the manager's office.

On the second day of his four-day trial, Richard made an unscripted appearance in courtroom number five when the jury was asked to watch the security video of him unloading his trolley in Tesco on 24 August. As the members of the jury concentrated on the flickering colour film that showed him unloading his trolley, Judge Michael Sachs quipped, 'It's certainly not going to get a BAFTA, is it?'

Richard smiled along with everyone else in the crowded courtroom. For two days he had sat impassively in the dock, his face barely registering a flicker of emotion as he listened to the evidence. It was the same icy calm he had been famed for throughout his professional life. And now here he was, on one of the most nerve-racking days he was ever likely to experience – smiling.

It was on day three of the trial that Richard finally got the chance to tell his side of the story. He told the jury that he had taken the wine and champagne out of absent-mindedness, not greed. He said his forgetfulness had become a bit of a family joke since he'd started working on *This Morning*, and that while he was perfectly able to focus his mind during his 90-minute live broadcast each day, he was incredibly forgetful in everyday life. He said that when the family had gone on a self-catering holiday in Devon, he had left two full bags of paid-for groceries at the check-out. 'It meant the family did not have much for dinner that night,' he laughed. 'I was not flavour of the month.'

When asked how solid his financial position was, he told the judge and jury that for the first time in years his finances were in a 'decent state'. He also said he did most of the family shopping himself, a habit he'd acquired back in 1985 when his wife was pregnant.

Finally the day of judgement dawned. As it had been for the past three days, the public gallery was crammed to capacity. But now tension rather than excitement gripped the hot stuffy courtroom. The fans who had sat for days listening to the evidence would finally discover whether their TV hero was a thief or not.

Even the barristers couldn't believe the extent of the public's interest in this minor case. Not when next door in courtroom number four there was the most appalling murder trial involving a nightclub owner who had had acid thrown in his face. This was usually the kind of gory case that drew the crowds, not one involving a minor shoplifting offence.

But what the legal eagles, some of whom had never heard of Richard Madeley before the case, hadn't grasped was that this wasn't just a shoplifting case – this was showbiz!

Judge Sachs began his summing up on Thursday 4 July at around 2pm. At precisely 3.10pm he sent the jury out to consider their verdict. It was 5.24pm when they slowly filed back to deliver it.

It had been a long hot afternoon in the airless room where the jury had sat trying to decide the fate of the man in the dock. For almost two and a half hours they had argued – and still reached no verdict on count two, resulting from the incident where Richard Madeley was filmed on security camera leaving the Tesco store.

The members of the jury filed back. Richard saw them come. He took a deep breath. The clerk of the court asked him to stand up.

The foreman of the jury was asked by the clerk if the members of the jury had reached a verdict on which they were all agreed on either of the two counts. The foreman replied that they had.

'On count one of this indictment, charging the defendant with theft, do you find the defendant, Richard Holt Madeley, guilty or not guilty?' asked the clerk.

The silence was deafening. No one moved, no one spoke. 'Not guilty,' said the foreman.

There was a loud murmur from the public gallery.

The clerk asked if that was the verdict of them all. The foreman replied that it was. He was then asked if the jury had reached agreement in respect of count two. The foreman replied that they had not.

Judge Sachs asked the jury to retire again to see if they could come up with a verdict upon which they were all agreed. If they could not, he said, he would then be prepared to accept a majority verdict of 10/2.

The jury retired for a second time at 5.26pm to return for the final time at 6.08pm.

This time the crowd in the public gallery felt sure they were going to get a verdict. They all leant forward and sat on the edge of their seats. The tension was palpable. Again the clerk of the court asked the foreman to stand.

'In respect of the second count of this indictment charging the defendant with theft, has the jury reached an agreement on which they are all agreed?'

The foreman said they had not.

The whole courtroom seemed to sigh out loud.

Judge Sachs intervened to ask the foreman a question. 'Could you just answer the question I am about to ask you "Yes" or "No"? If I gave you some further time, do you think there is any reasonable prospect of your reaching a verdict on which at least ten of you are agreed?'

'It depends on what you mean by reasonable time, your honour,' the foreman replied.

Judge Sachs asked, 'Is the answer "Yes"?'

The foreman of the jury answered, 'Reasonable as in . . ?' His voice trailed off. 'I would think not,' he said finally.

Judge Sachs asked if that was the view of all the jury. Silently, they nodded their assent. 'Very well, I discharge you from returning a verdict in respect of the second count. I am grateful to you for the trouble and attention you have given.'

So what did it mean? Was he innocent or guilty? Richard looked to his counsel, seeking the answer. The people in the public gallery didn't know what it meant either.

Within seconds, counsel for the prosecution, Mr Anthony Gee, QC, had risen to his feet.

'Your honour, the jury has been unable to reach a verdict on count two after this trial which has lasted four days. The prosecution in this, as in all cases, has to consider whether it would be in the public interest for there to be a retrial before another jury in the future. And, amongst the considerations of this case, the Crown has regarded not only for the *nature* of this charge and the character of the defendant, and in particular whether a fair retrial on the remaining count would be possible having regard to the press coverage this case has received.

'Having regard to all those circumstances of and surrounding this case, the Crown has come to the conclusion that it would not be in the public interest for there to be a retrial.'

Judge Sachs directed a not guilty verdict on count two. And the moment he did was the moment Richard Madeley's mask of impassivity was cast aside. He had been found innocent. The man who for four days had showed not one flicker of emotion could no longer contain himself. He kept punching the air with his fists and repeating, 'It's over, it's over.'

Outside the courtroom the press was clamouring for a reaction from the ecstatic couple, but Judy and Richard were taken straight to the Granada building, only moments away from the courtroom. By now Richard had abandoned any attempt to keep cool. He was totally hyped up – but happy. He was still like that twenty minutes later on that warm July evening when he and Judy gave a press conference inside one of Granada's great brick-walled warehouses.

There were about a dozen reporters waiting when Richard eventually made his appearance. He sat down at a polished teak table, flanked by Granada's head of publicity, Ian Haworth, and his wife.

'I don't know what the plan would have been if Richard had been convicted,' admits a member of Granada's press office. 'But there must have been one, which I suspect was known only to the people at the very top of Granada. Before the trial, I did ask if Richard would be fired if he was found guilty. The answer was no.'

But even five years after the trial that proved his innocence, Richard is still the butt of cruel shoplifting jokes. Just three weeks after he was cleared he became the victim of a smear campaign. Hundreds of posters proclaiming a spoof event called the 'Richard Madeley Sponsored Trolley Dash' were sent to colleagues of his. They were even circulated in pubs and clubs and police stations all over Manchester.

At the time Richard's solicitor, Michael Green, said he was sending a letter of complaint to the chief constable. 'While one has to have a sense of humour, it has to be weighed against the traumatic experience people go through in court,' he said. 'If we are to believe in our system of justice, when people are acquitted, at the very least they are entitled to enjoy that acquittal in peace.'

And there was more to come. In 1994, Bob Geldof took a dig at Richard when he appeared on *This Morning* as a guest. Richard was saying how surprised he was to hear that the musician had been declared bankrupt for a day.

The singer hit back and said, 'It's like shoplifting, Richard. I couldn't believe that either.'

Months later, a hoaxer calling herself 'Elizabeth from Yorkshire' phoned the programme saying she wanted to take part in a live phone-in. Instead, seconds after going on air, she said to Richard, 'Can I just say something, Richard?' Not knowing what was to come, he nodded his assent. 'I just wanted to ask whether you could steal me a bottle of wine from Safeway?' said Elizabeth.

The presenter was visibly shaken but, within seconds, had gathered himself and retaliated. 'I knew we'd get one of those one day,' he said with sang-froid. 'These are sad people. They're anoraks.'

Anoraks or not, it is clear that there are some people determined not to let Richard forget the past. After the trial he talked about the horror of having to live with being 'guilty by suspicion'. He said, 'Until you can prove your innocence, there's always a doubt above your head.'

If Richard Madeley thought the horror was over the day he walked out of Manchester Crown Court an innocent man, he was proved wrong. Because five years on he has learnt that even innocent men still have to live with doubters and detractors.

11 Sofa Wars

I T HAD BEEN DUBBED the 'War of the Sofas', the almost comical-
sounding fight for coffee-time TV supremacy. But when
Anne and Nick finally faded into mid-morning oblivion in
May 1996, it was the end of a four-year ratings battle that
had been conducted with acrimony and bitterness on both
sides. Behind the smiles of the opposing daytime duos a war
had been declared and lost. The conflict between the supremos
of morning television frequently took the form of hurtful
stories about the four personalities involved. But for all the
smears, one fact was clear: after its first two years on air *Good
Morning* never had a hope of catching its rival.

In reality, the ratings battle was won two years before Anne
and Nick finally threw in the towel. But it was only in March
1996, after weeks of uncertainty, that BBC1 controller Alan
Yentob finally decided to pull the plug on a show that had been
crippled by dwindling audiences and internal dissent.

The decision came as no surprise to everyone at Pebble Mill.
For months stories had been leaked that *Good Morning* was
not a happy ship. And Anne Diamond had cut her working
days from five to four.

For a programme that had been launched with much fanfare
and had confidently vowed to oust *This Morning* from the top
slot, it was an ignominious ending. For Richard Madeley and
Judy Finnigan, looking down from their £1.5 million perch at
Granada, it was vindication at last. 'They took us on, we saw
them off,' said Richard after the BBC finally capitulated and
announced that their show was to end. 'We shouldn't gloat, I
know. But we find it very satisfying.'

But back in 1992, when it was announced that Anne and

Nick were to host the BBC's daytime show, there had been eager anticipation throughout the industry. It had seemed an inspired decision to pit the golden couple of the early eighties against the golden couple of the late eighties.

Nick and Anne had a proven track record at TV AM, where their on-screen partnership had been credited with saving the station after a disastrous start.

The irony of this new development was that Anne and Nick first got the idea of doing their own daytime show when they were asked by Granada to act as holiday stand-ins for Richard and Judy. At that time Anne and Nick hadn't worked together since the demise of TV AM and felt this would be the perfect opportunity to see if the old magic was still there. The response from the viewers convinced them it still was. Hundreds of letters poured into the Granada studios, saying how wonderful it was to see the old team back together again.

Anne and Nick couldn't have been happier. They'd had a wonderful week, sparring with each other on screen. They'd forgotten how much fun it had been, sharing the sofa in the old TV AM days at Camden Lock.

Anne's producer husband, Mike Hollingsworth, had also wanted to know if Diamond and Owen still sparkled together on screen. Could their partnership still conjure up that old TV magic? After seeing them on *This Morning*, he was convinced that it could.

Anne and Nick's chemistry at TV AM was popularly credited with saving the ailing station after the much-publicised departure of the Famous Five – Anna Ford, Angela Rippon, David Frost, Michael Parkinson and Robert Kee.

Anne Diamond in particular swept through the Camden Lock studios like a breath of fresh air. She was bright eyed. She was bubbly. She was natural and wholesome. But it was that smile that really did it for Anne Diamond. With her chirpy, girl-next-door looks she was no great beauty, but that smile not only sliced through the dreariness of everyone's early morning, it rocketed TV AM through the ratings. People suddenly wanted to turn on their TV and brighten up their day with Anne Diamond.

Nick Owen was her perfect foil – the hapless, hopeless, henpecked 'husband' figure whose funny quips couldn't fail to put the viewers in a good mood. The couple's perceived strength was that they were neither glossy nor glamorous – this was Mr Ordinary and Mrs Average, a homespun antidote to the more polished presenters of whom audiences had tired.

After TV AM, the public didn't see Anne and Nick as a couple again until the idea for *Good Morning* was born. In the interim they had both married – though not each other – and had children, and Anne Diamond had gained a sympathetic following for the way she responded to her son Sebastian's cot death. On the face of it, they seemed like the ideal competition for Richard and Judy.

Mike Hollingsworth, Anne's husband, had first been approached by the BBC in 1991 to see what could be done about their almost non-existent daytime ratings. Miriam Stoppard and Adrian Mills, who had been dubbed 'Ms Haversham and Pip' by a *Daily Express* TV critic, had been presenting a programme called *People Today* which had barely made a dent in Richard and Judy's ratings. Granada were palpably racing ahead and to the outside world the impression was that the fusty old BBC was just eking out a bare existence during the day. It couldn't even enter the daytime war because it had no weapons to fight with.

Meanwhile, the slick husband-and-wife duo on the other side, in their cosy, brightly coloured studio, were dealing with the way ordinary people lived their lives – and pulling in an audience of nearly two million viewers while they were about it. That, coupled with the heady mix of their sizzling sexual chemistry and 'true life confessions' style of presenting, seemed to be exactly what the daytime viewer was looking for. The BBC knew they were going to have to do *something*. The question was, what?

Hollingsworth's initial reaction to the runaway success of *This Morning* was to advise the BBC to wave a large cheque book under the noses of Richard and Judy and try to tempt them away from Granada with bundles of money.

But if Mike Hollingsworth was aware of the appeal of Richard and Judy, so was Granada. As a company, it knows how to look after its stars, not just with fat pay packets but with a support system that extends far beyond the studio doors. Besides, both Richard and Judy had been with Granada for many years. They knew how the company worked and were grateful for having been given their 'big chance' there. And Richard and Judy both knew that with *This Morning* they were on to a winner. The other opportunities that would be made available to them because of it were just too exciting to walk away from.

For their part, Granada were determined to hang on to their two new stars. They were aware that the masterstroke had been to pair a real-life husband and wife on screen. The intimacy of the sexual and psychological relationship between two presenters was something that had never been fully utilised before in television. Richard and Judy were a compelling team, not just professionally but personally as well.

But what had become their biggest weapon in the sofa war was the way they exploited the 'that happened to us' factor. The shared jokes, the intimate exchanges, the personal revelations, all just 'happened' in the beginning. But as time went by Richard and Judy realised that this 'keyhole' into their lives was a big factor in the success of *This Morning*.

And so they opened up to their viewers. Richard told a vast network audience that he had had a vasectomy because their daughter Chloe had been unplanned and they were terrified of having more children. He talked about Judy's gynaecological problems. They both talked about their kids, their car, their money problems, and anything else that happened to come up. They flirted outrageously and fought regularly. Judy would tick Richard off it she thought he had gone too far. In reply he would tell her she was wonderful.

For the viewers it was real life gift-wrapped in the glamorous world of showbiz, and they felt genuine empathy with this couple they believed to be 'ordinary' – just like them. The success of the show was that it adopted the basic breakfast-time TV philosophy of a comfortable sofa environment, which to be fair Anne and Nick had made their own in the early-eighties, and ran with it.

The result was more of a *Dynasty*-style aspirational programme. It was flash, it was brash, and it was glossy. In magazine terms it was the equivalent of *Hello!*, but with Richard and Judy at the helm *This Morning* still managed to retain a northern feeling that kept the whole concept warm and approachable.

Even their co-presenters were different. These weren't the well-rehearsed, neutral-voiced types who were the norm in television in those days. Fred the weatherman, Mrs Brookes the cook and Denise Robertson, agony aunt, were not just unglamorous – they were unknowns.

It was during those very early days, as the programme steadily gained recognition, that *This Morning*'s bosses decided to make it a rule that if any presenter got above him or herself and became difficult or demanding they were immediately replaced. There was no leeway given to anybody who might imagine he or she was a bigger 'star' than someone else, or that the programme couldn't survive without him or her. No matter how good they were on screen, no matter how popular they might have been with the viewers, there was no truck given to temperamental presenters.

'If they were a nuisance they were got rid of,' says an ex-member of the *This Morning* team.

The reason for that, of course, was that *This Morning* was being produced on a shoestring. There was no money, barely any staff, and anyone who wasn't prepared to muck in with everyone else was simply a burden. But even when difficult people were told their contracts weren't being renewed, it was always interesting to see what kind of leaving party would be thrown in their honour.

An ex-presenter says that there would always be a little party at the end of a person's last programme, where a 'send-off' trolley laden with food and drinks would be wheeled into the studio. Exactly what was on the trolley depended on how popular the person leaving had been. If he or she wasn't particularly liked, there would just be a tea trolley with a few biscuits and cakes. If he or she was fairly well liked it would be a trolley with lots of wine. And if TV bosses were genuinely sorry to see the person go there would be champagne all round.

As with every company there were often grumbles among the staff at *This Morning*. But because no one could afford to be heard gossiping on the studio floor the place everyone went when they needed a smoke and a chat was a little glass-sided balcony that overlooked Fred's weather map. When things went wrong in the newsroom or in the studio, or if people simply wanted to moan and groan about their lot, you could always find a handful of them out on the balcony. No matter what the weather was like there would always be little groups of them huddled together smoking and complaining about something or someone.

'It was hilarious,' says an ex-presenter. 'The balcony was surrounded by glass which meant that everyone, including the bosses, could see whoever was out here.'

'And if people were out there you knew they were gossiping about something they shouldn't be,' says another ex-member of the team.

Mike Hollingsworth says that, looking back, the only chance the BBC had of winning the daytime war would have been to poach Richard and Judy from Granada before *Good Morning* ever went on air. 'But, of course, they ignored me when I told them.' By the time the BBC realised that Hollingsworth had been right and that Madeley and Finnigan were *the* couple in daytime television it was too late even to *think* about luring them to the other side. Granada had their golden couple in golden handcuffs.

The BBC went back to Hollingsworth and asked what they should do. He told them that, having missed their chance to buy Richard and Judy, who had achieved an almost 100 per cent share of the audience, they had to come up with a pretender to the throne. That 'pretender' had to occupy the same territory on the BBC as Richard and Judy did on ITV, which meant the programme had to go out at the same time on the same days and at the same time of year. Then, by stealth, it had to snatch the audience by gently tempting it away. In other words, the BBC should produce a copycat show that at first glance looked and sounded the same as *This Morning* but which, Hollingsworth believed, would eventually be a better quality programme than Granada's offering.

It was decided that the only way to beat Richard and Judy was to go up against them in head-to-head battle. 'The idea was that we would occupy some of their territory and, when we had a sizeable audience, we would move away – up, down or across the market, it didn't matter where – from being clones,' says Hollingsworth. 'That was the aim.'

The rekindling of Anne and Nick's on-screen partnership was conducted in a blaze of publicity. They were back, and the message was they were going to be big again.

So, on 11 October 1992, *Good Morning* went on air for the first time at the Pebble Mill studios in Birmingham. Backstage, some of the new presenters waited nervously to make their TV debut. The show's resident doctor, Park Porter, kept pacing the floor, repeating the speech with which he was to introduce himself to the viewers. New to TV, no one was more surprised than he when he'd turned up for an audition a few weeks before and been told he'd got the job.

In front of the camera, Anne and Nick were on a roll. They looked like they'd never been away. Unlike Richard and Judy, their chemistry wasn't sexual. In fact, in positional terms they were the polar opposites of their competitors. With Anne and Nick, it was Anne who was the aggressor and Nick who had a 'Yes, dear, I'm not going to argue with you' feeling about him. Whereas with Richard and Judy it was Richard who invariably took the conversational lead and, although she might slap him down now and again, Judy who remained the more reticent one.

But on that first morning, even though they were nervous, everyone could see that Anne and Nick were glad to be back together again. In the last-minute rehearsals before going on air they giggled and teased one another as they took their positions in the colourful TV living room which had dozens of framed photographs scattered everywhere and a neat row of kiddies' wellingtons at the fake front door. Nick and Anne were back where they belonged – together.

The big excitement that day was that Joan Collins was to be their star guest. She'd arrived not long before the start of the show, decked out in an exquisite black leather suit – a long skirt and short, skimpy jacket. It was just 10am, but in true soap diva style, Joan was coiffured and made up to the nines. And if she'd looked a bit too 'Hollywood' in the green room before the show, on screen she looked every inch the 'star'. Getting Joan Collins to Birmingham had been a definite scoop. Anne and Nick knew it. So did Richard and Judy. That first day *Good Morning* pulled in 1.2 million viewers.

It was a better start than *This Morning* had had five years before. Then their shows were averaging just 100,000 viewers in the first months and they hadn't had guests like Joan Collins. In fact, they'd had a hard job getting guests at all.

'After that first year we were clearly levelling with *This Morning*,' recalls Mike Hollingsworth. 'At the end of the 92/93 season we asked the Broadcasters' Audience Research Board to tell us how many people in the course of a week tuned into *Good Morning* and *This Morning* for a period of more than ten minutes. The figures showed that *This Morning* was achieving 10.4 million and *Good Morning* 10.6 million.'

Although statistics can prove or disprove anything, depending how you interpret them, the fact was that the first year of *Good Morning* was a successful one.

'We were very pleased,' says Hollingsworth. 'It was clear that *This Morning* had lost a million viewers and we had taken them. And, although Granada tried to rubbish what we had done, they were doing it in a way that clearly showed they were beginning to panic.

'Until we came along they'd had the patch to themselves, and although they'd created an excellent programme, they had done it in the teeth of virtually no opposition.

'But *Good Morning* got some very good stories that first year, including an interview with Stephanie Slater, the girl who was kidnapped by Michael Sams, who then met the wife of her kidnapper on screen.

'I think our audience didn't quite know what was going to happen when they turned on. There is a delicate balance that has to be achieved with a daytime magazine programme. The audience wants continuity and a certain amount of predictability, but within that they suddenly want their jaw to drop open and to think, My goodness, I didn't know that. They want to be able to say to people: "Did you see such and such on *Good Morning*?" I think it was clear that they [*This Morning*] wobbled very badly under our asssault that season.'

It was after that first year that the sniping and alleged 'dirty tricks' began. Both programmes were indulging in a fair amount of 'in office' tittle-tattle which would very often surface as a story in the press. If one side could find some way of interpreting the ratings that would be detrimental to the other, the story would immediately be 'leaked' to a newspaper. And stories about the presenters of both programmes abounded.

'It became very personal at one stage,' says Hollingsworth. 'There was a belief over at *This Morning* that staff at *Good Morning* were fuelling rumours. The fact was that we all knew that journalists were looking for anything they could get. They were like bees round a honey pot both in Liverpool and Birmingham at that stage. As far as I personally am concerned, I am not aware of ever having been involved in anything which was designed to denigrate the other side.'

Both couples suffered as a result of the so-called 'smear campaign'. There were totally unfounded stories about marital problems between Richard and Judy, and equally unfounded stories about the Hollingsworth/Diamond marriage being in trouble, as well as allegations of internal problems within the BBC and how it was not backing its daytime show.

By mid 1993 the smears and counter-smears had really begun to take hold in the popular press, although both sides were claiming not to be responsible. In a letter to *Broadcast*, television's trade magazine, Hollingsworth wrote: 'Put Richard and Judy up against some decent opposition and they squeal like stuck pigs.' The letter was to trigger off a whole year of very public controversy. 'I felt that Richard and Judy were behaving like spoiled children,' says Hollingsworth. 'Someone else was playing with their ball and they didn't like it. They had sat there for four years as the king and queen of the castle and they obviously found it irritating when somebody from the other side came along and stole their clothes. And that's exactly what *Good Morning* had done.'

The 'stuck pigs' quote caused an uproar. It was interpreted at Granada as a cruel dig at Judy's weight problem. But Hollingsworth denies this was the case. 'The phrase "stuck pigs" was an army phrase current during my childhood in a military family. The trouble was there were some people at Granada who thought I had chosen [it] very carefully, that, it was also an implication some people were slightly overweight.'

By 1994 the sniping had reached flash-point. There was a press conference for the autumn relaunch of *Good Morning* in September. By this time *This Morning* had left Anne and Nick behind in the ratings race. But still, Anne Diamond and Nick Owen stunned a roomful of showbiz reporters when they claimed their ratings were low because they had been victims of a 'dirty tricks' campaign aimed at sabotaging their show. 'Some of it has been quite hurtful,' said Anne.

She and Nick told the assembled reporters that smears were coming out of the *This Morning* camp centred around rumours that there was a rift in the Diamond/Hollingsworth marriage, and claims that a 'crisis' meeting about the show had been chaired by BBC1 controller Alan Yentob. But Diamond was careful to make it clear that her remarks were not directed personally at Richard and Judy. 'It's nothing personal with them,' she said. 'They probably feel as bad about it as we do.'

The accusations were like a gift from God to the showbiz hacks who had trudged along to the press conference that day wondering what they were going to get out of it. As far as they were concerned the ratings war had been well and truly won by Richard and Judy, yet this outburst from Anne and Nick showed that they still had some fight left in them.

The journos got a story they'd never expected in a million years and the following morning Anne Diamond's sensational claims made headlines in almost every newspaper. The tabloids revelled in all the bitching and backbiting over the coffee cups, the sofa showdowns and sniping behind the smiles. If the talons were out between the daytime duos, the press was going to make sure everyone knew about it.

More than 495 column inches were devoted to Anne's 'dirty tricks' allegations in the *Daily Mail*, *Daily Mirror*, *Today*, the

Daily Telegraph, and the *Guardian*. Even columnists Lynda Lee Potter and Anne Robinson followed through with a few sharp jibes.

On the basis that 'there's no such thing as bad publicity', the 'dirty tricks' stories got *Good Morning*'s new season off to a pretty spectacular start.

But despite the brouhaha, Granada decided to play it cool. They could afford to. After all, they were beating *Good Morning* out of the water. Dianne Nelmes, by then controller of factual programmes, said she was 'saddened' by Diamond's comments. 'All this talk of dirty tricks is masking one simple fact,' she said. 'And that is *This Morning* has dominated the daytime audience for six years because it delivers a stunning programme to its audience.'

But still the sniping continued. There were stories that one camp had tried to woo guests away from appearing on the rival programme. Film director Michael Winner, who had always refused to travel to either show unless he had a film to promote, said publicly he finally chose to appear with Richard and Judy as opposed to Anne and Nick because *This Morning* had agreed to send a satellite van around to his home in Kensington so that he could do the interview in his own back garden. 'I didn't do *Good Morning* because I didn't want to travel to Birmingham and the BBC didn't offer the satellite van,' he said at the time. There was talk of inducements to guests from both sides: chauffeur-driven cars, first-class rail tickets and even private planes. Celebrity guests were always being asked by journalists which show they liked best and further fuelling the rivalry.

But if the sofa wars seemed all-important to the players involved, there were others in television wondering what on earth all the fuss was about. Daytime television was only ever watched by between three and five million people – and that was at peak times. Out of a total television audience in Britain of 45 million people, the five million daytime audience was chicken feed.

More than that, a study by the ITV Network Centre showed that people were pretty half-hearted about their daytime viewing habits anyway. They watched both magazine programmes in the same way as they listened to radio shows. They'd tune in while they were wandering round the house doing other things, or else stop and watch for ten minutes or so while they had a coffee break. And even then they *still* weren't over-enthusiastic about what they were seeing. Data from the Harris Research Bureau in 1995 showed that more than two-thirds of viewers had criticised the daytime schedule for being of poor quality, while only a piddling four per cent believed that daytime TV fare was of high quality.

Even one of TV's top executives, Andy Allan, Carlton's director of programmes and the man who was one of the original members of the Daytime Committee that commissioned *This Morning*, slated daytime TV in the *Daily Mirror* in 1995 as 'a dull and predictable wasteland'.

'I watched a lot of coffee-time TV during a stay at a health farm,' said Allan. 'And it was a bit like being in a flotation tank robbed of all sensory perception. Shift workers and those who are housebound should qualify for a special allowance for watching it.'

It was a scathing attack, but according to Harris it was representative of the general feeling. The evidence was clear that no matter how good *This Morning* and *Good Morning* were, neither programme was good enough to make people rearrange their schedules. No one was going to stay at home to watch if they had planned to go out. More tellingly, they wouldn't even stop what they were doing at home to watch. 'Only ten per cent of the population is ever at home during the day,' says ratings expert William Phillips. 'That is a total of five million people. But, of those, only between two and three million people will be watching television. Everyone else is either out shopping or doing other things. Both *This Morning* and *Good Morning*'s audience is so tiny it is hardly worth talking about. Everyone says Richard and Judy are massively successful because they can pull in 1.7 million viewers at peak time, but in prime time a show that pulls in less than five million is slated as a flop.'

Phillips insists that the daytime shows should be viewed as

part of the overall viewing picture. 'Vanessa Feltz, who has a talk show in the afternoons, regularly pulls in two million people every day,' he says. 'That's because more people watch TV in the afternoons because they have done what they needed to during the day and they are settling down in the afternoon to relax a bit.'

But he says *Good Morning* never stood a chance of winning the ratings battle against Richard and Judy. 'In recent years *This Morning* has always had a crushing advantage. The BBC's mistake was to play two programmes of the same kind off against each other. *Good Morning* was never going to catch up with Richard and Judy because *This Morning* got there first. They had a four-year head start.

'The real genius of *This Morning* was to have a married couple presenting the show, and if the BBC were so prepared to copy the format they should have competed with another married couple. Richard and Judy are also superb at what they do.'

TV insiders believe the mistake *Good Morning* made was to adopt an entirely different atmosphere from the cosiness of *This Morning*. 'The trouble was they created the wrong tone,' says a BBC source. 'And the viewers did not like to hear technicians guffawing in the background every time the presenter made some kind of joke. Viewers do not like jokes they can't share and don't want to hear backstage people laughing like jack-asses, especially when they know they are being paid to do it.'

It was also thought that because Anne and Nick's 'season' was often interrupted by party conferences and special schools programmes, there wasn't the same continuity that Richard and Judy enjoyed. *Good Morning* could only come back on air in October once all the party conferences had finished, which gave *This Morning*'s viewers a month's head start to rediscover and reassert their loyalty.

'Anne and Nick were often handicapped by the BBC's public service commitments,' says an insider. 'Which meant a lack of continuity. The viewers took their cue from that and believed that, if the BBC didn't think *Good Morning* was good enough to stop interrupting it with other programmes, then neither did they. And they switched to the other side.'

The harsh truth was that, even though the two shows were identical in many respects, the public preferred Richard and Judy to *Good Morning*. In the last couple of years of the BBC show's run, ratings consistently showed that *This Morning*'s share of the daytime audience stayed at around 60 per cent to *Good Morning*'s 40 per cent.

'But this ratings thing must be put into perspective,' insists William Phillips. 'Richard and Judy average out about 1.5 million viewers at their peak time which is about 11.30am. But those figures are only for about two minutes. The rest of the time it sticks at about one million. Nick and Anne's figures were between 700,000 and 800,000 at peak time.'

It was always difficult to assess exactly why one programme was perceived to be better than the other, bearing in mind they had almost identical slots and, on some days, identical items. It was much more the fact that Richard and Judy's show was seen as being slicker than Anne and Nick's. There was also the unquantifiable 'cosy' factor. Viewers probably felt more comfortable with Richard and Judy. Judy's patent openness and sincerity are the Madeleys' trump card. As well as coming across as a focused and capable journalist who asks the questions everyone wants to hear the answers to, she is a motherly figure and an obviously loving wife as well. Her forte is not the soft interviews she and Richard do with visiting celebrities – where she comes into her own is when she is talking to ordinary people who have extraordinary stories to tell. Then she is capable of showing real empathy and sympathy without being patronising. She has shed real tears in the face of tragedy and laughed heartily when there is a joke to be shared. She listens, she feels, she understands.

PR supremo Max Clifford, who has been a guest on *This Morning* several times, says: 'The deciding factor for me has always been the quality of interviewing. I was approached by someone on *Good Morning* for an interview with Antonia De Sancha but it was obvious to me that they didn't really understand the subject.

'On a more personal level I think that Richard and Judy's appeal is that they are natural and not in the least patronising.'

Judy Finnigan will openly admit that she is working class and born in a two-up, two-down *Coronation Street*-style house. Until they bought their new London residence, Richard and Judy lived in an ordinary house in an ordinary street in Manchester. They didn't party or socialise with the stars. They bought pizzas and stayed home with the kids.

Anne Diamond, on the other hand, always came across as more brittle and more middle class than her *This Morning* counterpart. Unlike Judy, she openly admits to being ambitious. She's Pony Club as opposed to Working Man's Club, and the Warwickshire manor house she shares with Mike Hollingsworth is as far away from *Coronation Street* as it is possible to get. She was once described in her youth as 'every suburban mother's dream daughter', but today Anne Diamond lives an impressive lifestyle by anyone's standards. Perhaps some viewers found it more difficult to relate to this woman, whose life they felt they could never be part of.

Judy Finnigan's life, on the other hand, appears to be an open book. She's warm, she's working class, and although she has recently moved to a £700,000 house, it's taken her a long time and a lot of hard work to get there. She isn't 'to the manor born', she worked her way there.

Richard Madeley just seems to have been born to be a successful TV presenter. Lesley Ebbetts, fashion editor on *This Morning* for seven years, says of him: 'He has the common touch. He can make everyone, from Barry Manilow to a little child, feel comfortable. I don't know how much of this is contrived but I think after eight years we would have seen if it was. What you see is the way he is.'

Whatever the secret of *This Morning*'s success, the fact is that in television terms the ratings are still pitifully small. And it is perhaps the low ratings which have been largely responsible for the show's lack of superstar guests – not the often quoted reason that they would have to travel up to Liverpool.

Says one TV insider: 'It isn't that celebrities didn't want to travel north because it was too far. It was because, once they got there to promote their new film or book or TV show, they were only going to be seen by a maximum audience of 1.5

million. Their agents would just tell them to forget daytime and concentrate on the prime-time chat shows where they can have an audience up to ten million.'

If Richard and Judy were ever upset by allegations of 'dirty tricks', they kept silent – publicly at least – until 1996.

'We had nothing personal against Anne and Nick,' said Richard then. 'But we kept hearing quotes from them, saying they were going to wipe the floor with us. But it didn't happen.'

Anne Diamond gave her press conference, Richard and Judy made their feelings known, but actual encounters between the four principal players in the controversy were assiduously avoided. Anne and Mike and Richard and Judy have not been in the same room together for years, let alone spoken to each other. 'Although I wouldn't feel uncomfortable if we were,' says Mike Hollingsworth. 'But there has never been an occasion when we were able to or when it would have been proper to accept an invitation. There have been some surreptitious attempts to invite Anne and me to something where Richard and Judy would also have been. It would have made a good story, I suppose.'

But even if he does not see much of TV's golden couple, he says he still likes them and rates them both very highly as professionals. 'There is absolutely no doubt that Judy Finnigan is extremely popular. People like her because they feel she is reflecting their own demeanour and I feel it is such a shame that the newspapers have made such a big thing about her weight. As long as she continues to do what she does with panache and style, why should she be pilloried for what is purely a physical characteristic?

'As for Richard, it would be wrong to say I dislike him. I admire them both very much, and I admire the show. Personally I think the star is Judy. There is no doubt the main audience of that show is the women who identify with her. They quite like Richard, they quite fancy him, but she's having to deal with him and what the viewers like to see is the way she deals with him.

'The fascination of *This Morning* is the relationship between Richard and Judy. I think a lot of women are fascinated by that. The fact is, he's a younger male who's not bad-looking. I think the viewers like to see how another woman deals with that situation because we are very rarely allowed to eavesdrop on how other people live.'

In the end, all the analysing, emulating, bids for scoops and competition for press coverage culminated in one simple fact: the outcome had become inevitable for a programme that, save for its first twelve months on air, was never any serious threat to the other side. *Good Morning* might have won a few battles but *This Morning* won the war.

The king and queen of daytime still reign supreme. The question is: for how long?

12 It'll Be All Right on . . .
This Morning

W
HEN *THIS MORNING* first hit our screens back in October 1988 it was barely expected to survive its first nine-month run. It had two unknown presenters, an untried and untested magazine format and an unquantifiable element called the 'cosy factor' which programme bosses were gambling on being *the* component to revolutionise daytime viewing.

Who could have imagined that, nearly ten years on, *This Morning* would be the most successful and talked-about show on daytime television, and that its presenters would be hailed as the undisputed king and queen of their medium, earning a gigantic £1.5 million a year between them?

It seems barely believable that come September 1998 *This Morning* will be celebrating ten gloriously successful years. It's been a decade of highs and lows, of laughter and tears. There have been items that were hilariously right, others that went disastrously wrong. There have been scoops that made national headlines and clangers which did the same. But the most crucial and fascinating aspect of the *This Morning* story is that no one ever got bored. Here is a programme that has not only carved out for itself a place in the annals of TV history, but has stealthily imprinted itself on a nation's consciousness. *This Morning is* daytime television – the lodestar around which all the other shows revolve.

Now, as the programme races towards its tenth anniversary, let us look back on some of its most memorable moments – the fun, the fights, and also the flops. Let's look at what happened when the glamour and the gloss slipped, to reveal chaos and confusion. Who were the people keeping it all together? What were the things the public sensed but never saw? Because if live television generates an electrifying energy for those who work within it, it also generates sheer terror at the things that can, and frequently do, go wrong.

This Morning is more susceptible to these gaffes than most because of the sheer number of television hours it must fill. There is no other live daytime or evening show that runs for as many hours a week. In fact, the first week *This Morning* was on air, the team drank gallons of champagne at the end of it to celebrate the fact they'd got through five days without having the plug pulled on the show.

'It was, and still can be, a technical nightmare,' says a member of the team. 'In those early days some of the crew had never done a live show before and they knew they had to get it right because they couldn't go back and do it again.'

But even that first week had its share of disasters. One of them was a fashion item that Judy was doing with the then fashion editor, Lesley Ebbetts. The blonde presenter was standing in the colourful studio with her back to the area where the models were supposed to be coming out on to the studio floor. The idea was that the girls would do a few quick changes backstage and then walk towards the camera.

'The trouble was,' says Lesley, 'one of the models actually got stuck in her clothes and because Judy was standing with her back to this girl, she couldn't see what was happening. I, however, could see it all. But since I was doing a commentary on the clothes, the only thing I could do was keep talking about what the model in front of me was wearing. I couldn't let her walk off because there was no one else ready to come on. I kept droning on about what this girl was wearing and Judy was looking at me like I'd gone mad. I was trying to catch her eye to signal how frantic I was. In the end I walked over to her and very gently moved her towards the area of the set where the girls were changing.

'Bless her heart, she realised immediately what was happening and we were both able to ad lib our way out of it. But from then on it was a rule that presenters always had to be sitting facing the action so they could see when anything was going wrong.'

Richard and Judy fast gained a reputation for making people 'confess' their innermost secrets on screen.

In February 1984, after years of rumour and innuendo, DJ Alan 'Fluff' Freeman finally admitted to Richard and Judy that he was bisexual. Appearing on the show, the then 66-year-old Radio One presenter said that though he'd been celibate for twelve years, he had previously had lots of problems with his sexuality.

'I had quite a go from the age of twenty on both sides of the fence,' he said. 'I had a whale of a time.'

He even joked with the two TV presenters and told them, 'If I was confronted with either of you when I was thirty, I wouldn't know quite who to chase.'

'Fluff', who had once been engaged to a model but who for years had batted off rumours that he was gay, was asked by Richard and Judy if he was homosexual, bisexual or heterosexual. 'I'm just me,' he said. 'I enjoy being with whoever wants to be with me, provided I want to be with them.'

Freeman's confession, which had been extracted both gently and good-humouredly by the two presenters, set the pattern for the programme's interviews. People who agreed to be interviewed by Richard and Judy immediately felt they could confide in this sensitive young couple who were a refreshing antidote to the more hard-nosed ladies and gentlemen of the national press.

The impression Richard and Judy gave their guests was that a trouble shared was a trouble halved. It was a formula that brought them exclusive after exclusive, not least when in December 1995 they interviewed Stephen West, the son of evil Fred and Rosemary West, whose horrific murders at 25 Cromwell Street had shocked the world.

Stephen had agreed to give his first-ever interview to Richard and Judy and talked movingly about how he and his sisters had coped with the horrors of their childhood. As he talked Richard and Judy could barely contain their own emotion, especially Judy who, with tears in her eyes, told Stephen at the end of the interview: 'I wish you all the luck in the world with the rest of your life.' Richard, seeing his wife's distress, reached out to comfort her and told Stephen, 'A good and happy life from now on. You certainly deserve it.'

Their trademark warmth was a characteristic for which they were later to be criticised when they tried to use it to the same effect on their prime-time chat show, the *Richard and Judy Show*. Then their interviewing technique was slated for being too soft and non-confrontational for a prime-time audience. But it was exactly right for the daytime viewer. No one wanted to see guests 'savaged' in the interests of truth at 11am while they were having a coffee break. They didn't want to see that nice Mr and Mrs Madeley turn into hard-faced, hard-nosed interviewers, sacrificing sensitivity to get at the truth.

But as well as more sensitive and emotive issues, *This Morning* has also focused on news and current affairs. They've tackled the problems that surround teenage sex, abortion, single mums, relationships between parents and children.

One of their most memorable campaigns was to look at the plight of the children in Romanian orphanages. 'We did a whole series of films in Romania,' says an ex-producer. 'The images of those children didn't just move the public, they got to everyone here as well. It was some of the most emotional footage we had ever screened.'

But if the news and current affairs items gave the programme gravitas, it was the behind-the-scenes bloomers, and the way Richard and Judy handled them, that made jokey headlines.

Like the time in April 1993 when Richard was chatting to the programme's wine expert, Charles Metcalfe. The two of them were sitting at a dining table which had been specially set up in the studio, discussing the merits of various foods and wine while sipping chilled champagne. The elegant scene was suddenly shattered when Richard, arms flailing and in a flurry of rude words, lost his balance and crashed to the floor.

The embarrassed presenter only just managed to avoid covering himself with the curry he had been nibbling a few seconds previously. But he did manage to drench his pristine white shirt with champagne.

Charles Metcalfe, who had watched Richard's tumble in

open-mouthed amazement, made no attempt to hide his fit of giggles.

It took a stunned Richard a few seconds to see the funny side of things but once he did he first of all apologised to viewers for his fruity language and then looked into the camera and asked, 'So where's Dennis Norden?'

For the *This Morning* team it seemed there were some days when a devilish little virus got into the machinery – because the same day that Richard took a tumble from his collapsing chair there were a series of other glitches: phone-in callers couldn't get through, live links broke down and Richard's microphone went off midway through an interview.

Just a few weeks after the incident with the champagne there was another technical gaffe which plunged the entire studio into darkness just at the moment when Richard and Judy were conducting an interview with *Peak Practice* star Kevin Whateley. The couple were talking to Kevin, who had finished working on *Inspector Morse* with John Thaw and had landed the role of a country doctor in a new series which was later to become a smash hit.

For Whateley the interview was an important one as it was arguably the first time he had had to 'carry' a major series. But just minutes into their chat the lights in the studio suddenly began flashing on and off. Richard, determined that the interview should carry on, apologised to Whateley and then shouted over to the panicking crew: 'Leave the lights – we'll carry on in the dark.' And they did, which meant that Whateley was able to plug his new series and Richard and Judy had once again triumphed over disaster in the world of live TV.

But in April 1994 Richard came up against something which turned out to be a tad more difficult to deal with than flickering studio lights.

Hercules, the 8ft showbiz bear, was visiting the *This Morning* studio with owners Andy and Maggie Robbin, who told Richard that their big ol' grizzly was so tame that once, when he was lost in the Hebrides, he almost starved to death because he was too gentle to kill even a rabbit.

But what no one told Richard was that even tame bears get

hacked off when a human looks like he might be about to pinch their lunch!

Andy and Maggie were just telling Richard how Hercules scoffs £140-a-week's worth of food, his favourite being Marks & Spencer's chicken which he was enthusiastically tucking into that morning on the show. And that was where Richard made his first wrong, and potentially catastrophic, move. Lulled into a false sense of security because Andy and Maggie had assured him that Hercules was a big baby who wouldn't hurt a fly, Richard reached out to stroke the bear's nose just as it was having its lunch.

In a terrifying instant Hercules lunged towards him, sharp fangs bared, and looked momentarily as if he was prepared to sacrifice his M & S chicken for a large chunk of Richard's hand.

Understandably the presenter was shaken and visibly struggled to compose himself as the realisation of what might have happened suddenly hit him. But even in his state of shock Richard managed to pull himself together enough to joke, 'I'm sorry, Hercules. I was only asking what that scar was on your nose.'

'It isn't just Richard who has had to cope with embarrassing moments – Judy has had her fair share, especially at the hands of her own husband who just can't seem to keep quiet about what goes on behind their bedroom door. Like the time he told millions of viewers about his and Judy's attempts at the rhythm method of contraception and how they had failed because of the irregularity of Judy's ovulation. For once Richard's revelations about their private life had gone too far and his wife's scarlet face registered her fury. 'Do you mind?' she hissed at him through clenched teeth.

And if it wasn't bad enough that her own husband talked about their sex life in front of two million people, Judy also had to cope with some of *This Morning*'s guests taking an interest as well.

There was the time back in September 1993 when America's most famous sex therapist, Dr Ruth, gave Judy step-by-step instructions on air about how to keep Richard happy in bed.

As a disbelieving Judy sat dumbstruck, Dr Ruth Westheimer told her: 'Maybe you could do this tonight, Judy. Sit up and watch Richard and every 90 minutes you will see some kind of erectile activity. You can cure this by making sure you have sex with him during the evening.'

And just to make sure that Judy had got the message, Dr Ruth went on, 'But if he does wake up aroused, bring him to orgasm very fast. You just make all the movements for him but don't talk. Then turn over and go to sleep.'

Judy, who could hardly believe her ears, had been blushing furiously the whole time Dr Ruth had been speaking. With an embarrassed giggle she told the sex therapist, 'I really don't think so.'

Richard, a smile plastered across his face from ear to ear, wasn't the least bit embarrassed and said to his wife a few minutes later, 'Remember, love, it's every 90 minutes.'

And just to unsettle her even further, he added, 'Or maybe we could go for the record and make it every 70 minutes.'

By this time Judy had had enough and snapped back at him, 'Oh, shut up. You're making me very embarrassed.'

Despite the fact that many of the glitches that occurred on _This Morning_ were because of technical problems, there was still the human element that went way beyond the control of anyone or anything at the Albert Dock.

Like the time Richard and Judy had just handed over to Fred on his weather map. As the boisterous forecaster hopped about on the floating map of Great Britain, enthusiastically predicting a warm day with lots of sunny spells, a saucy scouser called Mark Roberts suddenly leapt into view.

Completely naked, Roberts sprinted across the map towards Scotland as a dumbfounded Fred tried desperately to carry on with his forecast. Back in the studio, Richard and Judy were helpless with laughter and as fascinated as everyone else about what was going to happen next.

Determined to get maximum exposure, Roberts, who had been banned from every football ground in Britain because of his bare-bottomed antics, then tried to make a flying leap from Scotland to Ireland on the map. Whether it was nerves or the excitement of hearing cheering from people on the dockside, he suddenly lost his footing and plunged into the freezing water.

Back in the studio Judy was wiping away the tears of laughter from her eyes. 'I haven't had such a good laugh in weeks,' she said.

And it wasn't just Judy who was feeling a whole lot better for the 'Roberts' experience. The streaker also made a big impression on one of the programme's guests that day, Mandy Smith, who suddenly lost all interest in promoting her new record and preferred instead to talk about the relative merits of Mark's backside. Afterwards Roberts's explanation for his unsolicited streak was that he likes making people laugh. 'I knew Fred's weather map was seen all over the country so I couldn't miss the chance to put a smile on the faces of millions,' he said. 'I wasn't worried about Richard and Judy. They have a good sense of humour and they loved it.' Talk about bare-cheeked face!

But even if Richard and Judy weren't too put out by what had happened, *This Morning* bosses, who had blocked out the streaker's naughty bits on screen with a *This Morning* logo, were less than delighted. 'It's not something we would want to happen,' said a spokesman.

If weatherman Fred imagined that having his forecast sabotaged by a streaker was all the excitement he was going to get for one week – he was wrong. Just 24 hours later there was another calamity just waiting to happen.

Hollywood action man Dolph Lundgren, who was a guest on the programme, had agreed to join Fred on the weather map. In an effort to make things a little more dramatic than usual, programme bosses had agreed to let special effects men rig up a few smoke bombs and detonators to make the forecast go off with a bang. Only things didn't just go with a bang – they went up in flames as well, when a bundle of camouflage netting lying over the Scottish hills dramatically caught fire after the first explosion. Fred and Dolph immediately sprang into action and managed to dampen the flames before they engulfed the entire map.

'It just wasn't Fred's week,' said a spokesman for the

programme later, in what must have been the understatement of the year.

One of the most talked about incidents on *This Morning* happened in January 1996 when *Pie in the Sky* actresses Maggie Steed, who plays Margaret Crabbe in the series, and Bella Enahoro, who plays Detective Sergeant Cambridge, gave Richard and Judy a public dressing down for making a series of on-air gaffes about their show. Maybe it was because it was the second day of the New Year that the atmosphere in the studio that morning was particularly tense. It was Richard and Judy's first day back at work after the Christmas holidays and the two actresses didn't seem to be in the best of spirits either. But as the interview progressed it became clear that Richard and Judy had never watched *Pie in the Sky* before. Whether they hadn't seen or assimilated the information in the programme notes before the show isn't clear. But what did become clear was that the actresses were irritated by the presenters' lack of familiarity with the programme they had gone on *This Morning* to talk about.

When Judy first described *Pie in the Sky* as a sitcom, Ms Steed rebuked her by saying: 'You have obviously not watched it. The show is not a sitcom. It's a comedy drama.' Things got worse when Richard then made some comment about how detectives had 'terrible home lives' and Ms Steed, who plays the wife of Detective Henry Crabbe, replied, 'I take great offence at that. He has a very, very happy marriage.'

At this point Judy came to her husband's rescue and asked Ms Enahoro if she had been in *Pie in the Sky* since the first series. 'Yes.' replied the actress sarcastically. 'I think we've got an inkling that you haven't been watching.' Judy then tried to cover her embarrassment by saying, 'Bella, I believe you've got a degree at Cambridge, haven't you?' To which she replied, 'No, actually, I'm going to Cambridge to study at the end of this year.'

Realising there was no possible way to retrieve the interview, an annoyed Judy said, 'I think our information is worthless,' at which point Richard exasperatedly screwed up his research notes and threw them away. 'It's our first day back after

Christmas, I'm afraid, and we don't know where we're at,' he confessed.

Then, as a dig at the researchers and production staff, he pulled his eyelids down to look hungover and said, 'Honestly, you should see the team.'

The incident left a bad taste, but it was unusual. Richard and Judy generally get on well with most of their guests, save for the embarrassing incident with Sir Bob Geldof. There was also a bit of on-air sparring with Richard's current affairs hero Robin Day, and some friction when *Darling Buds of May* star, Pam Ferris, who had purposely put on two stone for her role as Ma Larkin, accused Judy and Richard of being responsible for a 'gross joke' when she went on their show and discovered a huge plateful of cakes had been left beside her during a chat on dieting. 'It suggests large women can't control their eating habits,' she said later.

But even if Richard and Judy have liked most of their guests, there have been some they liked more than others. Robert Powell was one of their big favourites, as were Cliff Richard and Cilla Black.

Another charmer was *Cracker* star Robbie Coltrane, though when he appeared on the show he wasn't looking his best, says a researcher who was working on the programme that day. 'Robbie had agreed to be on the show and because *Cracker* was top of the ratings at the time it was thought to be a bit of a coup. He arrived in Liverpool by helicopter that morning but when he stepped out of it his dark designer suit was covered in white powder. He had brought his young son with him on the plane and the little boy had tipped a whole tin of talcum powder over his dad. But Robbie wasn't the least bit cross. He was totally charming to everyone and great fun too.'

People who have worked on the *This Morning* team for any length of time are familiar with what have become known as 'Richardisms'. These occur when Richard says something that seems quite innocent to him but which can be interpreted in a totally different way by the viewer.

One such incident happened recently when the presenters were doing an item about diet fads. Richard and Judy had interviewed the slimmer of the year and she had been asked to stay on and do the phone-in. Judy was talking about some dietary gimmick when suddenly, out of nowhere, Richard piped up: 'Do you know, the most fattening thing a woman can ever ingest is sperm?'

There was a horrified silence in the studio. Judy's mouth dropped open. The phone-in guest looked gobsmacked. And up in the gallery the editor of the programme, Geoff Anderson, was already on the phone, asking, 'Did he say what I think he just said?' Anderson's worst fears were confirmed.

Says an ex-member of the team, 'What Richard had meant was that sperm makes women pregnant, and therefore it makes them look big. But the whole thing came out appallingly badly. But then, that's a typical Richardism. They are hilarious.'

One of the most chaotic days on *This Morning* happened about three years ago when, for a whole segment of the programme, Richard and Judy actually went missing. *This Morning* was into its final fifteen minutes, during which time Fred was to do the weather and Richard and Judy were to introduce a trapeze artist who would perform for a few minutes then come down from his swing to talk to the two presenters. It should have been simple.

Says an ex-producer of the programme: 'The plan was that Richard and Judy would do a live link into the break then they would jump into a waiting care outside the studio which would take them to the other side of the dock where the trapeze artist was waiting to do his stuff.

'The problem was there was a new floor manager at the time and because she wasn't too familiar with the layout of the dock she sent the car to completely the wrong place.

'By this time the commercial break was over. Fred had done his weather and Richard and Judy were supposed to be at the foot of the trapeze, waiting to introduce the "flyer" and ask him what he was doing in Liverpool. Only they weren't there. More importantly, no one had the vaguest idea where they were.

'So the producer got a message through to the technicians on the dock who told the trapeze artist to start his act. While this was going on, the viewers could just about catch glimpses of various *This Morning* crew members frantically waving their arms about in the background.

'By now the trapeze artist who had been swinging around for all he was worth was about to finish, and still there were no presenters to talk to him. So he got a signal from one of the crew on the ground that the second he was finished, he was to start the whole thing over again and keep going until someone told him to stop.

'In the meantime everyone was going crazy trying to find out where Richard and Judy had got to. Suddenly, the sound man had the amazing idea of fading up the microphones so we could hear Richard and Judy and work out where they might be. Unfortunately he did this on air and out of the blue came their voices shouting. 'It's over here!' 'No, it's not, it's over there.'

As soon as the sound man realised that millions of people were being treated to the sound of the two presenters arguing about where they were supposed to be, the microphone was hurriedly faded out.

The upshot was that the viewers didn't get to see Richard and Judy for the remainder of the programme. They were missing for more than ten minutes and eventually the closing credits were rolled with the trapeze artist still swinging.

'The phones were going crazy after the programme,' says a member of the team. 'Because the viewers hadn't seen Richard and Judy for more than ten minutes they assumed something terrible must have happened – that they had fallen into the dock or something. We had to reassure everyone that they were alive and well.'

The problem was that, while they might have been well, Richard and Judy were definitely not happy.

'The poor old floor manager, who was brand new, was absolutely mortified that she'd sent the two star presenters haring round the dock on a wild goose chase,' says an ex-producer. 'But eventually, because she was so new, she was forgiven.'

Another time that a technical glitch had viewers rolling in the aisles was when Fred the weatherman was doing some kind of stunt with a fake canoe. The idea was that at some point in the programme viewers would hear the *Hawaii-Five-O* theme tune and Fred, pretending to paddle, would gently glide across the TV screen. But of course he wouldn't really be paddling. The canoe had a rope attached to the front of it which was to be pulled by a man at the opposite side of the studio.

'Well, Fred, being the professional he is, decided to have a practice session before his big moment,' says one of the show's ex-producers. 'So he started waving his arms about in a paddling motion. The problem was that the man with the rope at the other end of the studio saw this and thought all this arm waving was his cue to start pulling. So he hauled Fred across the studio floor, right at the moment when Richard and Judy were doing a link about something terribly serious and poignant. Suddenly, out of nowhere, comes a grinning Fred, paddling for all he was worth, to the tune of *Hawaii-Five-O*.

'Well, Richard and Judy just collapsed into a fit of giggles. There was nothing else they could do, having been confronted by this incredibly surreal spectacle of Fred sailing across the screen in his canoe.'

Almost everything Richard and Judy do is guaranteed to make headlines. Which is why when Judy turned up at the studio in September last year with a black eye, having stumbled into a mantelpiece, programme bosses realised they were going to have to give viewers an explanation.

Judy would have been quite happy to let her make-up people do their job and carry on as if nothing out of the ordinary had happened, but Granada executives were astute enough to know that the press could make a very big deal out of a black eye. So, after a stream of phone calls, it was decided that Judy would have to tell viewers what had happened.

After a few quips about bondage sessions and having a touch of the 'Lon Chaneys', she finally confessed that she had bumped into a mantelpiece at their rambling Victorian home in Manchester.

'That's what you get for tidying up after your children,' she said, referring to the fact that she had apparently been cleaning her daughter Chloe's bedroom when the accident happened.

But if Judy wanted to play the incident down, the *This Morning* team had no intention of letting her.

'What on earth have you been doing to her?' said the programme's cook, Susan Brookes, to Richard, when she saw Judy's shiner.

Dr Chris Steel, *This Morning*'s resident GP and the man who has dispensed medical advice to thousands of people over the years, hit the headlines himself in 1996 when he made the brave decision to talk about his own skin cancer on air. His courage in talking about the disease helped thousands of viewers come to terms with their own problems. He even asked his cancer specialist if *This Morning* cameras could film the surgery to remove his tumour so that viewers could watch and then take better care of their own skin. 'I don't want to frighten people,' he said. 'I want to reassure them that it's nothing to worry about.'

Chris blamed his own foolishness as a teenager for the cancer. He says he used a sunlamp to treat his acne but sat in front of it ten times longer than he should have done.

In its nine years on air *This Morning* has had some intoxicating highs and some dispiriting lows, but it is perhaps because there have been so many more highs than lows that the show has always maintained its 'feelgood factor'. *This Morning* has assumed a life of its own and become a creature which thrives not just *because of* but sometimes *in spite of* everything it creates.

Whatever happens to the programme in the future, whether it fails to find a new home in London or whether it flourishes and soars to even greater heights, one thing is certain: *This Morning* has a glorious and distinguished history, and in the dull, predictable world of daytime programming it is something of which its creators and the people who made it work can be proud.

13 The Future

J UDY FINNIGAN STEPS OUT of the family car and bustles her children past a pack of waiting press photographers. Head bowed, she pulls her coat tightly round her and then, wrapping a protective arm around Jack and Chloe, deftly steers them through the chaos of popping flashbulbs into the relative privacy of their new London home.

If Judy felt exposed in her bikini on that beach in Antibes, everyday life in a city that seems endlessly fascinated with the minutiae of her life must be a whole lot worse. But then, this is everyday life in the capital for a prime-time TV star. Maybe if she'd known it was going to be like this she would never have left the relative privacy of Manchester where people knew her well enough to leave her alone.

But how could Richard Madeley and Judy Finnigan ever have imagined that a city with more journalists, paparazzi and picture agencies than the rest of Britain put together could ever be a safe haven from the press?

How could a couple who have always professed a need to be ordinary, to stand back from the razzamatazz of television, willingly transport themselves and their family to a city that is obsessed with the fame game?

The fact that they splashed out on a £700,000 Hampstead house and moved their entire lives south was not just to do with Hollywood stars refusing to travel to Liverpool for *This Morning*. They wanted bigger and better challenges than *This Morning* could offer.

For years the couple had felt they were stagnating in Liverpool, and the only way to change that was to move to a city where the streets were paved with prime-time opportunities.

Eight successful years at *This Morning* had given Richard and Judy considerable clout. They had money. They had position. They had security. The only thing that still eluded them was prime-time success. That's where the real power was and neither of them was going to be happy until they had it. Instead of being watched by just two millions housewives each day, Richard and Judy's ambition was to be seen by more than ten million viewers.

So why this insistence that they are, and will remain, ordinary?

'There is no danger that we will lose touch with whatever normality we have,' said Richard in 1996. 'We will not become luvvie-ish because we're just not like that.'

But perhaps Richard and Judy don't see that they may already be in danger of losing touch with 'normality'. They have chauffeur-driven cars laid on for them. Few challenge their authority on *This Morning*. People are automatically deferential to them.

Rachel Purnell, who used to work with them at Granada in the eighties and is now senior vice-president of editorial at MTV, says that fame generally changes people. 'Television presenters suddenly realise they have power and want everything done their way. Fame means they suddenly start having nice things done for them. They have cars sent for them, they have people to do their errands, and eventually they lose touch with reality because they don't have to deal with the problems relating to their own lives. They just say to some minion 'Get my life fixed for me' and it's done.

'They get caught in the trap of craving the fame, but at the same time keep banging on about how much they want their privacy. It's an extraordinary thing to watch and, although it may seem like a sweeping generalisation, I can't actually think of a single presenter it hasn't happened to.'

Richard has said publicly that the move south doesn't mean he and Judy are suddenly going to become London socialites, hobnobbing with the rich and famous at an endless round of parties and premières. However, many of his colleagues believe that once he experiences the star-studded lifestyle of the capital it can't fail to be of major interest to a man who has spent ten years living quietly behind closed doors.

Friends say Richard and Judy know precisely why they are going to London, and it's not to be 'ordinary'.

'Richard wants to be an international star,' says someone who has worked with him, 'and he knows you can't be an international star in Liverpool.'

If this is true then the move to London would make perfect sense because a bid for international stardom can only be made from the capital.

The move, and the launch of the new evening show, meant that Richard and Judy had to make the public newly aware of them; to publicise themselves all over again. In the first six months of 1996 the couple did more interviews with newspapers and magazines than they had in the previous four years. It was the first step in a plan that they and Granada hope will catapult them from the relative obscurity of daytime to the powerful world of prime time. If they are to attract millions of viewers who have never heard of them before they need exposure in the press. They need to tell people who have never watched *This Morning* who and what they are. But, in doing so, it may prove difficult, if not impossible, to maintain their presentation of themselves as 'ordinary people'.

Prime time is not peopled by Mr and Mrs Average. Its presenters are high-energy, high-profile and highly paid stars. If Richard and Judy want to be among their number, it follows that things will have to be changed after their previous forays into prime time.

But no matter how much weight or money Granada throw behind the Madeley/Finnigan partnership, there are those who believe they would have been better off sticking exclusively with their daytime audience. For them, the much-hyped interview with O. J. Simpson on their debut 7pm slot was proof to some that Richard and Judy just do not have what it takes to make the transition into prime time. Despite weeks of publicity, promoting them and their infamous guest, the first programme of their *Richard and Judy Tonight* series and its two presenters were slated. 'Richard and Judy Guilty' screamed the headlines the following morning; 'Chat Show Couple Let O.J. off the Hook'; 'The No Punch and Judy Show'.

In fairness to them, Richard and Judy had fired all the right questions at O.J. Simpson – they just didn't come close to eliciting the answers everyone wanted to hear. It was never O.J. who looked to be under pressure. Instead it was Richard and Judy who looked terrified throughout the entire interview. Judy's hands shook uncontrollably and her upper lip quivered. Her husband, who looked only marginally less nervous, asked questions that were easy for Simpson to evade. Each interviewer continually interrupted the other.

'As interrogators go, Richard and Judy came and went more like Eeyore and Piglet than Paxman and Humphrys,' said the *Daily Telegraph*'s Nigel Reynolds.

Richard hit back angrily at the critics. 'We promised to ask the questions that everyone wanted to hear – and we did,' he said. 'Did we tailor the interview to demonstrate prime time toughness? Twaddle! We approach all interviews, daytime or prime time, on their merits.'

And it was perhaps unfair to expect that in twelve minutes two television presenters could succeed in eliciting any fresh insight into a character as baffling and contradictory as Simpson's. There was also the fact that the basic chemistry of such an encounter was never going to succeed. Though found innocent of murder, Simpson's history of domestic violence was still fresh in the public's consciousness. It was, therefore, always going to be an uneasy mix: a happily married couple interviewing a man known to have been aggressive towards his murdered wife.

In the event, if the O.J. interview proved anything it was that while Richard and Judy are capable journalists, critics expect something less lightweight for prime time. 'It was not a brilliant start,' says ratings expert William Phillips. 'Why do people have to get greedy? Why don't Richard and Judy stick to what they're good at? And what they're good at is daytime television. They made two fundamental mistakes on that show. They shouldn't have had a guest like O.J. in the first place. And if they were going to talk to someone appearing for the first time on British television, they should have given him more than twelve minutes. During the day they interview people tactfully and respectfully and they get a lot out of them. Why don't they stick to that? People seem to have forgotten that they have had one prime-time chat show that flopped before. As far as I can see the formula for this one is exactly the same. They haven't learned from their mistakes.

'Anyway this whole business of bringing back the chat show is nothing to do with what the public wants. It's to do with the state of the finances of television companies. Chat shows are cheap, and they keep trying to revive the format because if it did click it would save them so much money. But the fact is they haven't clicked. Part of the trouble these days is that people who go on chat shows are so well drilled they never give anything away. And anyway, it's usually only the B-stream stars that appear on chat shows. I mean, when did you last see Clint Eastwood appear on one?'

But perhaps the real test is the ratings. That first show in the *Richard and Judy Tonight* series pulled in just seven million viewers. It was a disappointing start considering that the game show it replaced, Phillip Schofield's *Talking Telephone Numbers*, regularly pulls in audiences of between eight and ten million.

Whether or not the move to London will prove to be a disaster or a success for Richard and Judy, it is one which has been on the cards for years. But it was certainly interesting to watch over the first half of 1996 their newfound openness with a press who in the past they have steadfastly avoided. It was also surprising just how openly and frankly they talked in those interviews about their very personal lives – about rumoured problems within their marriage, problems concerning the eight-year age gap, Judy's battle with her weight, Richard's ambition – and perhaps it was a measure of their determination to establish themselves in the city they hope to make theirs.

It was all a very marked contrast to the previous Liverpool years when a job in the Richard and Judy press office was known as the 'graveyard shift'. Says one former *This Morning* employee who worked there for more than a year: 'At first you thought, What a great job! And then you realised there was no point whatsoever in approaching Richard and Judy to do interviews. We would get daily phone calls from newspapers and magazines, and all of them were so desperate to get an interview that they would promise picture and copy approval. But Richard and Judy just weren't interested.'

In April 1996, however, the couple talked frankly about their press phobia in an interview with the *Daily Telegraph*. When the interviewer suggested they might have had a *little* bit of flak from the press, Richard exclaimed, 'A little bit? It's like flying over the Ruhr in 1944.'

In that same interview Judy said that she had been 'gobsmacked' by the malicious publicity she and Richard had been forced to deal with in recent years. She has said that although she isn't naive and to some extent understands the press and public's interest in her life and especially her marriage, she cannot come to terms with the fact that what has been written about her is unbearably voyeuristic.

But perhaps it *is* naive for anyone who appears on television for 90 minutes, five days a week, and gets paid £1.5 million for their trouble, to expect either anonymity or privacy? Both Richard and Judy know full well that one of the pivotal reasons for their success is the fact that they are a married couple who are very much in love and make this apparent on screen. In fact, it was they who 'sold' their on-screen relationship to Granada bosses right at the very beginning of *This Morning*, on the basis that they were a couple and the combination was so unusual it was bound to be a ratings grabber.

But the public's curiosity about this couple cannot just be put down to the myriad press stories that have been written about them. Richard and Judy themselves must bear some of the responsibility for it. Every day on *This Morning* they give away little insights into their very private lives – their children, their health, the state of their finances. Even their sex life and method of contraception have been up for discussion. Such insights have become part of the fabric and format of the show. And presumably they give away these snippets about their private lives in the knowledge that it is what attracts viewers. Of course it is understandable that they crave privacy, but, having given away so much of themselves, they surely cannot entirely blame the press and public for wanting more?

Many who have witnessed at first hand the effects of fame on Judy feel that she has become very cautious and at times overwrought by the pressure of work.

'She has become dependent on Richard,' says an ex-*This Morning* producer. 'If Judy has a problem she gets Richard to sort it out for her. If there is something she's unhappy with it's *him* who often fights her battles. While once Richard might have spoken on her behalf, or on behalf of them both, he now just does *all* the talking. Judy has either forgotten how to or she has allowed Richard to take over.'

But maybe her reluctance to deal with situations at work and her habit of letting Richard talk on her behalf is due to the fact that as a couple who have become a finely tuned and professional unit, they have fallen into a pattern where one automatically lets the other deal with situations that present themselves. Perhaps Judy understands that as the calmer, more even tempered of the two, Richard is perfectly adapted for dealing with situations that she finds difficult. So it's not so much a case of him fighting her battles, but him dealing swiftly and smoothly with a situation that could spiral out of control. The fact that Richard appears to have become more assertive since the start of *This Morning* could be because he has assumed more responsibilities, not just on his own behalf but on his wife's as well.

'Richard is the one who makes the decisions in their lives – both editorially and personally,' points out a Granada insider. 'Everyone has a huge respect for Judy, especially her interviewing technique. She's direct, she's intelligent and she's incisive. Richard is the less effective of the two. But if you ever ring her at home, she will put him on the phone straight away. It's as if she doesn't know what to say without him.'

Or maybe it's not that she doesn't know what to say without Richard, more that she believes he handles things better than she does. It is accepted within Granada that the balance of power within their relationship has shifted in recent years. In the beginning it was Judy who called the shots. She was older than him, more mature, and he was absolutely besotted by her. But these days it is Richard who, maybe because he has been able to accept and deal with the implications and the complexities of fame more easily than his wife, has taken control.

Those who know Judy say this is no great hardship for her, because while she enjoys being sexy and clever for her man, she is still old-fashioned enough to want him to be in control. She believes she cannot do what she does without Richard and sees him as the coper in the relationship. It is a role that Richard enjoys but none the less one which may have brought about unfair criticisms about his Svengali-like control over his wife.

The crushing work schedule of the past eight years has also had its effect on Judy. Says an ex-member of the *This Morning* team: 'Judy is one of those people who instinctively knows when something has gone wrong off camera. She has this incredible antenna which can work for her professionally, but it can also work against her because she is worrying all the time about things she doesn't need to worry about. It always amazes me how calmly she comes across when she is asking questions because we all see how tense she is. It registers in her body.'

Colleagues have been seeing the strain Judy is under for some time. She worries about the smallest things – a hair being out of place, someone dropping a coffee cup at the other side of the studio. Even someone in her eyeline at the back of the camera is a source of stress to her. While Richard seems to thrive on the inevitable crises that accompany nine hours of live television every week, they are taking their toll on his wife. In the last couple of years there have been occasions when Richard has had to present the show on his own because Judy was ill at home.

'I think she's fed up with the pace,' says someone who has worked closely with them. 'She wants to be at home with her kids but she know she has to carry on because of Richard and her fans. It's what drives her to go on.'

There are many who believe – rightly or wrongly – that Judy has been persuaded to go to London by her husband, who realises that as a TV couple they have a limited time left on screen. If Richard is ever to strike out and make a career of his own, the time and the place to do it is now and in London.

Says Mike Hollingsworth: 'I am convinced that one of the major reasons behind this move to London is Richard. I think he realises that as a pair he and Judy have a limited shelf-life. I also think that Judy would probably rather be at home with the kids. My feeling is that another year or so will go by, Richard and Judy will consolidate *This Morning*'s success, and then I think there will be an attempt by the two of them to break free.

'Judy has done a very successful series of Sunday morning discussion programmes on her own. If Granada have any sense they will find her a good show that goes out once a week. It doesn't necessarily have to be prime time. But when she's on her own, she's very good.

'As for Richard, maybe something like *Newsnight* beckons or London will be a launch pad for America.'

There are many others in television who believe that Richard has now had enough of recipes and needlework features and wants to work at the hard news end of television.

'I cannot believe that the man who presents *This Morning* is the man I was married to,' says Richard's ex-wife Lynda Madeley. 'When I knew him he loved hard news and current affairs. He was a serious journalist. I can't imagine he enjoys talking about women's clothes and recipes. I always believed he would do well but I didn't think he would make his name on a programme that was watched by housewives. The man I knew wanted more out of his TV career than that.'

All of which might explain why Richard was determined to move to London and why his wife, despite her own reservations, was willing to go with him – not for the advancement of her career but for his. There is no doubt that at present people appear on the show and confess all, particularly to Judy. The question is, how effective would each be without the other?

In recent interviews Judy has said that, while she feels stifled and stressed by fame, she feels that living in London will ease some of that pressure. It is a notion based on the assumption that, because there are so many more stars living and working in the capital, two more TV presenters won't make much difference. Will Richard and Judy soon discover this is not the case?

Surely if they had wanted anonymity and freedom from press intrusion, they would have stayed in Manchester where, despite occasional outbreaks of interest, they were left largely alone? Had they come to prominence fifteen years ago in Manchester, when every newspaper office had legions of reporters and photographers on the pay roll, it might have been a different story. But the depletion and shutdown of many of those newspaper offices has meant that there is neither the manpower nor the resources to spend too much time on the Madeleys while they were north of Watford Gap. In London, however, where freelance reporters and photographers are plentiful, it is a different ball game. If a newspaper wants a story about Richard and Judy, unlike the skeletally staffed offices in Manchester, it will have the money and manpower to make sure it gets it. The paparazzi will also be keeping an uncomfortably close eye on TV's squeaky clean couple to see if either of them does anything to contradict their image. Far from being more anonymous, their exposure to publicity will be dramatically increased.

In April 1996, when the two of them travelled to London for the BAFTA awards, having been nominated for the award for Best Chat Show, they decided to make a weekend of it by taking Jack and Chloe with them. Judy later told colleagues excitedly how wonderful it had been to take her children for a walk in Hyde Park because no one recognised her. No one even looked at her. But surely she can expect that to change if she and Richard are successful in their quest to become prime-time celebrities?

And even if Judy doesn't fully understand what the move to London means in terms of exposure, her husband surely must. 'Richard will be in his element at all the celebrity parties,' says a producer who has worked with him. 'But he's going to have a hard time getting Judy there.'

The same producer says that the big city will be a total culture shock for the two stars who have had it mostly their own way at Granada. 'I think they are going to find it hard in London for a number of reasons. The first is that, until now, they have been big fish in a small pond in Liverpool. It's going to be very difficult in London where there are a whole lot of fish very much bigger than them. How are they going to feel when they walk into LWT and find they're in a queue behind Anthea Turner and in front of Cilla Black?' A top ITV insider said recently: 'Richard and Judy were at a big celebrity gathering recently. Richard looked like he was having the time of his life but Judy looked less comfortable.'

But if the personal readjustments of living in London are going to be hard for Richard and Judy, it is the professional ones that will make or break them. Critics say neither has what it takes to be a prime-time presenter.

A producer who worked with Richard while he was at Yorkshire TV says, 'The thing that always summed Richard up for me was the word "Lite". You know you have Lite cigarettes and Lite beer? Well, that's how I'd describe Richard. He's a very good very polished, "Lite" presenter.' Of course, that 'liteness', that smooth, reassuring manner, is actually a great gift and has ensured *This Morning*'s success.

Says another TV executive who has worked with them both: 'They are just too entrenched in what they do on daytime TV. When you do a programme that goes out at 7pm it has to have an incredibly high-energy quotient. It is a totally different pace to daytime TV and the problem with Richard and Judy has been that when they have had a crack at prime time they have been unable to adjust to that fast pace.'

At the time of writing, the evidence has backed up fears that Richard and Judy will not be a huge prime-time success. Their *Get a Life* health show in 1995 pulled in just six million viewers, while their prime-time Sunday night series, the *Richard and Judy Show*, was dropped after only one series. Says someone who worked alongside them on the *Richard and Judy Show*: 'No matter how many times we said to them, "Hey, guys, this isn't 10.30am on a wet Wednesday morning, it's 7.30pm on a Sunday night" it made no difference. They turned everything into daytime television.' Even their new *Richard and Judy Tonight* show, slated by the critics, is reported to have been dropped from certain ITV regions. TV chiefs have now decided that instead of it being shown nationwide it will only be screened in the Granada region, and although Granada insist that no firm decision has yet been taken on a second series of the chat show, the ratings speak for themselves. The first *Tonight* show attracted just seven million viewers and after that the ratings went into a decline.

The *Richard and Judy Show* was cancelled amid allegations that the interviewers had been 'too soft' on their guests. And they'd had very good guests. They were the first to get a face-to-face interview with Roy Cornes who, knowing he was HIV positive, had had unprotected sex and infected a number of his girlfriends with the virus. Afterwards Richard and Judy were pilloried by a disbelieving press and public who felt the man who had effectively sentenced these women to death received too easy a ride.

There was also criticism for their interview with David Mellor's former mistress Antonia De Sancha, who got off lightly despite the fact she had been publicly savaged elsewhere for her handling of the Mellor affair.

Jane Hewland, who worked with Judy at Granada many years ago and now runs her own production company in London, says: 'I'm not sure if they will work in London. The trouble is, when you base your career on a double act, what happens if that relationship falls apart? Will the public ever be able to accept either of them in a solo role or in anything that is not daytime?

'Judy is an excellent interviewer and she leads *This Morning*. If they turn out to be successful in a peak-time slot it will be by virtue of her. But the trouble is they have tied themselves to a marriage and a programme and that is going to be very hard to escape from. The public pigeon-hole people. If you're a star in one programme, that's where they like you to stay. They probably won't like Richard or Judy to be anywhere else but *This Morning*.

'And the battle Judy faces is that the public still judge people on the way they look. It's not fair but they do. Judy will not be the exception to that rule. The only women who succeed as they get older are women with a fantastic sense of humour – women like Cilla Black. Judy doesn't have humour. She's the straight woman and where's the space for straight women who are getting older? They do an Oprah Winfrey-type programme or they do daytime.'

If Richard and Judy *do* manage to change their style and become accepted as prime-time presenters, one TV insider believes that change will turn their core daytime audience against them.

'They've backed themselves into a corner by going to London,' he says. 'They will have to tread a fine line if they want to keep all their balls in the air. Yes, they have to change their style to make a success of prime time, but if they change too much and start coming across as sharp, hard-hitting, born-again sophisticates for the peak-time audience, how can they still be that nice ordinary couple who used to sit in Liverpool and sympathetically relate to people and their problems?

'I think this move to London and prime time may cost them both dear, which would be a shame because what they do on *This Morning* is brilliant. They are at their very best when they are talking to ordinary people with extraordinary stories to tell.'

There is no doubt that Richard and Judy will have a big battle on their hands in the capital. Even Ben Frau, who is a very good friend of the couple's, now a producer at GMTV, believes the move to London will be fraught with difficulties. 'I'm not sure if it will be good for them,' he says. 'I think part of the magic with Richard and Judy is that people don't know much about them. They are just two ordinary people who come into our houses every day. But in London they will both be constantly in the media spotlight and I think some of the mystery will disappear.'

There is also the fear that *This Morning*'s famous 'cosy' factor could disappear in the move to the new location. Anyone who ever went to the *This Morning* studio in Liverpool at the Albert Dock understood at once that it was different from other TV studios around the country. The team weren't just a group of people who worked together. They were a community, many of whom had worked on the show since day one. There was a feeling of togetherness there that the transient, ever-changing studio personnel in the south can never hope to recreate. In London people work on a programme for a while and then move on. In Liverpool people rarely move on because there are few other places to go.

Says Ben Frau: 'The Liverpool studio was a magical place. A lot of people were there since the year dot and for many people *This Morning* was so much more than a job. It was their life. Granada might not be able to bring that to London. It's a little bit of magic that just happens or it doesn't. In Liverpool it happened.'

Lis Howell, director of programmes at UK Gold and Living, says she doesn't know if the move to London is the right one for the show. '*This Morning* has got a fantastic shelf-life, but I think it's losing faith to bring it out of Liverpool. Maybe that's because I'm from Liverpool but all those people at the Dock who worked on the programme for years were what made it the success it is. They were all warm-up men. From the drivers to the make-up girls to the women who made the tea, these were the people who gave the place atmosphere.

'Maybe it *will* turn out to be a good move. It still doesn't stop me thinking it's a sad one.'

And if Richard and Judy want privacy in the big city, they have chosen the wrong place to live. Hampstead Garden Suburb is not only one of the most well-known residential areas of London, because of the many wealthy celebrities and business people who live there, it is also one of the most expensive. Having said that, rumours that the couple paid £1.2 million for their new home were wildly exaggerated. It cost £700,000 – still three times more expensive that their house in Old Broadway but by no means unusual for the area. Richard and Judy bought the detached house for cash after just a single viewing. It has eight bedrooms, four bathrooms, a family room, breakfast room and drawing room, lush split-level garden and a pretty summerhouse. There is also a granny flat on the ground floor with its own living room and bedroom.

Judy was upset when the press published a photograph of the house before the deal was even finalised. But it was unlikely to affect her decision to go ahead and buy because she fell in love with the house at first sight. So much so that the deal was finalised in less than five days.

Vanessa Feltz, who lives close by, is surprised at their choice of area. 'I would have thought they'd have gone to live in Weybridge or Berkshire because Hampstead Garden Suburb is a very North London Jewish area. I'd say 75 per cent of the people here are Jewish, and while of course Richard and Judy will be made to feel welcome, it just seems a strange choice for them.'

Some believe Richard and Judy chose the suburb because it nestles on the edge of Hampstead Heath and, although it is predominantly an area for the rich, it is also an area for families with young children. It is not the super-rich area of Hampstead proper, but still they will be living among bankers, lawyers, company directors – people who can afford the best of everything.

Their decision could also have been influenced by the fact that Hampstead boasts some of the best schools in the country. Always conscious of saving money, the couple could do no better than try and get nine-year-old Chloe down for the Henrietta Barnet school which is widely regarded as one of the best girls' schools in the country. It is also non-fee-paying. They might look too at South Hampstead High School for Girls, a public day school with only moderately expensive fees.

For Jack, University College School in Hampstead would be perfect.

Says one of the local residents, 'Jewish people tend to be very cliquey but they can also be quite star-struck. I think everyone will enjoy having Richard and Judy here. We are a community where the neighbours all know each other. I'm sure people will go out of their way to make the two of them feel at home. Whether they will like that is another matter.'

But in London in 1996 Richard and Judy can no longer hide behind their image as an ordinary married couple trying to bring up their children in a confused world. The truth is that today they are rich beyond the dreams of their viewers, and lead reclusive lives fearful of public attention and press intrusion. Already isolated from old friends, they now face a future in their high-security London home, separated from everything that used to be familiar.

Daytime viewers might well be convinced that they know the real Richard and Judy. But as the couple forge ahead, turning their backs on Liverpool and the formula that has worked so well for so long, do Richard Madeley and Judy Finnigan still recognise themselves?